VOICES OF ALOHA:
Remarkable People of ALOHA

Norm Bezane

(This is the sixth edition of the popular Voices of Maui series incorporating new tales as well as classic ones from an earlier volume, Maui for Millions)

VOICES OF MAUI SERIES ON CONTEMPORARY MAUI

VOICES OF PARADISE
PARADISE PEOPLE
MAUI TALES FOR MILLIONS
VOICES OF MAUI
MAUI CHRISTMAS 2012

COVER

Malihini Keahi Heath, long-time concierge at the Kaʻanapali Beach Hotel, "the Most Hawaiian Hotel."

Copyright, 2010, 2012, 2013 Voices of Maui Talk Story, LLC Published and distributed by Voices of Maui Talk Story, LLC, 156 Kualapa Place, Lahaina, Maui Hawaii 96761 June, 2013 ISBN:

In Hawaii we greet friends loved ones and strangers with ALOHA, which means LOVE. ALOHA is the key word to the universal spirit of real hospitality which makes Hawaii reknowned as the world's center of understanding and fellowship. Try meeting or greeting people with ALOHA. You will be surprised by their reaction. I believe itit is my creed. ALOHA to you.

Duke Kahanameka
Six- time Oympic Swim Medalist 1913-1924
Ambarassador to the World

Seattle embraces ALOHA.

THE AUTHOR AND ALOHA

WRITING PROFILES FOR LAHAINA NEWS, -more than 150 of them-on the remarkable people who live on or visit Maui, it has gradually dawned on the author that what they all have in common in the best sense of the word (not a tourist slogan but a way of life) is ALOHA.

ALOHA today can be found more and more on book titles. Yet, aside from words about what people think ALOHA is, few if any accounts include contemporary stories of how people live ALOHA every day. If ALOHA were an island, its capital building would at the Kaʻanapali Beach Hotel—known as the Most Hawaiian Hotel—in part because it is a place of ALOHA.

The author spends considerable time writing and meeting people there for just this reason..

Not a few visitors have told me that they could stay anywhere at the highest priced or most prestigious resorts. But they return again and again to the modestly priced KBH.

My favorite mentor there is Concierge Malihini Heath who is readily available to consult on things Hawaiian and recently added to my own perspective from 27 years as a visitor and 12 as a resident on the subtleties of ALOHA.

We begin Voices of Aloha with the people of the Kaʻanapali Beach Hotel ohana (family). And we move to others who live in the rest of Kaʻanapali and Lahaina.

A...lo...HA. You have heard it as a luau begins, at music venues, at ice cream parlors and ABC stores. You have heard it as a three-syllable word. And most likely, if you are a true believer, you pronounce it softly, as ALOHA in one breath. Some argue there is no one way to pronounce ALOHA, but I would beg to differ.

ALOHA is not an affection. It is real. Despite the popular bumper sticker, ALOHA is not practiced. It is lived and comes from within. ALOHA is empathy for others that resides in the heart and it can be acquired naturally if given a chance. ALOHA can take the form of a smile, a friendly manner or an act of kindness.

Growing up in Hawaii in cherished na ohana (family groups) Hawaiians learn ALOHA by example in youth and see it flourish in adulthood. Newcomers can become persons of ALOHA too and many do. ALOHA is an acquired approach to living equally available to those of us who live here who are passionate about Maui and Hawaii, to newcomers, and to visitors who catch the spirit.

ALOHA however isn't automatic. There are *some* Hawaiians (those with Hawaiian blood) who find the concept of ALOHA alien. You see it sometimes in an attitude when tied up in traffic, vying for coveted beach parking, or as a chip on the shoulder from perceived past wrongs.

The good news is you can find ALOHA without even looking for it. ALOHA is one of the things that make Maui and Hawaii so special. ALOHA is just one of many of the island's gifts to the world.

For those who want to know more about who we are , Voices of ALOHA includes a number of brand new profiles as well as classic older ones, and is also presented for the historical record. For these are among the very few accounts of the movers and shakers of the last several decades who have and continue to shape the new Maui.

TABLE OF CONTENTS

ONE

ALOHA AT THE MOST HAWAIAN HOTEL   3

THE CONCIEGE:
Malihini Heath
Ka'anapali Beach Hotel
Bringing the Spirit of ALOHA Alive

THE HOTEL KEEPERS:
Mike White/Lori Sablas
The Ka'anapali Beach Hotel
Becoming "The Most Hawaiian Hotel"

THE ULTIMATE VISITORS:
Chris Marcotte/Gary Bodine
Her Ashes Will Be Here Forever

THE BARTENDER:
Dale Simonsen
The Tiki Bar
Simply Dale

THE CRAFTSMAN:
Mika Villaran
Funny Fabulous Basket Maker

THE CARVER:
Funaki Tupoa
Tap, tap, tap and more

THE NEW PROPRIETOR:
Bonz Heath
Lahaina Spice Company
Spice it up

THE PREACHER:
Laki Ka'ahumanu
Church on the Go
From Green Fields to Saver of Souls

THE ENTERTAINER:
Alaka'i Paleka
KPOA
Morning Goddess: Missionary Of Music

TWO

ALOHA IN KAANAPALI   40

THE SERVER:
Christina Olayan
Leilani's on the Beach
Spills, Tears, Onward and Upward

THE CHEF
CJ (Christian Jorgensen)
CJ's Comfort Zone Deli and Diner
Getting Comfortable on Maui

THE ARCHITECT:
Uwe Schulz
Unsung Hero

THE CATAMARAN CLAN:
 Jim Coon
Trilogy Excursions
Cinnamon Buns and Band of Brothers

THE REALTOR:
 Bob Cartwright
Whalers Realty, Inc.
Provider Of Dreams Does More Than Sell

THE AUTHOR
Norm Bezane

THE MASCOT
Kea Aloha
Day in the Ka'anpali Life

THREE

ALOHA IN LAHAINA 82

THE HOSTESSS:
Laura Blears
Kimo's Restaurant
Famous Surfer to Hostest with Mostest

THE PARROT MAN:
Brian Botka
PURRFECT Days in Paradise

HISTORY PRESERVER:
 Jim Luckey
The Lahaina Restoration Foundation
A Luckey Lahaina Tale

THE MERCHANT:
Jim Killett
Lahaina Galleries
Artful Journey

THE ARTIST:
Jim Kingwell
Kingwell Island Art
Painting the Town Red, Green, Yellow and Blue

THE POP ARTIST:
Davo
From Hippydom to Pop Artist

THE RENAISSANCE MAN:
George Kahumoku
A Grammy Award Winner Lights A Fire

THE OLD TIMER:
Sammy Kadotani
OK, OK, the Man Who Can't Say No

THE **CULTURAL ICON:**
Charles Kauai Ka'upu 1957-2011
The Passing Of A Legend

FOUR

ISLAND HERITAGE 126

THE KING:
Kamehameha I
Kingdom of Hawaii
Warrior, Unifier, Surfer, Trader
Shaper of Maui

SEAMAN, AN AUTHOR, QUEEN AND KING Captain James Cook, Mark Twain, Queen Kaahumanu, King Kalakaua

DANCERS AND SINGERS
The Hawaiian Islands
Queen, Uke, Hawaii Calls, Slack Key Guitars

ONE

ALOHA AT THE MOST HAWAIIAN HOTEL

Hawaiians always have been people of ALOHA. It can be found in the old texts. It is one of the first words we learn to read. It starts as a greeting but takes on the meaning of a commitment. I can see it in people coming here for many years. It changes their lives. You don']t have to shout out ALOHA.

Malihini Keahi Heath
Concierge

THE CONCERGE:
Malihini Keahi-Heath
Ka'anapali Beach Hotel
Bringing Spirit Of ALOHA Alive

MALIHINI—Hawaiian for newcomer to the land—has an apt name. The concierge extraordinaire at what is properly billed as the most Hawaiian hotel, Malihini Keahi-Heath brings the spirit of ALOHA alive to other na malihini: first-time and longtime visitors to the Ka'anapali Beach Hotel (KBH).

Named after an area in Moloka'i (her grandfather was a Kupuna, or spiritual leader there), Malihini is descended from a great-grandfather who came here from Tahiti in 1708. Her eight brothers and sisters have led a different life than their parents.

Malihini's dad, a fisherman known as "Uncle Moon," worked for many years for Pioneer Mill, planting and harvesting cane starting at 6 a.m., running heavy equipment and eventually moving up to supervisor. Off at 2:30 p.m., he'd take a break, have an early dinner, and be off to Napili Kai Beach Resort to perform as a musician until 10 p.m. on many nights.

Mom, known as Auntie Primrose, had a florist shop in Lahaina and used to buy turtles and filet them in her back yard. Three of her eight brothers and sisters, including a musician, are involved in the visitor industry. Her five children include a hotel engineer, waiter, and dispatcher. Her new husband "Bonz," for many years a chef, now runs the Lahaina Spice Company, the two opened in 2012. Bonz got the nickname because he was so thin. Originally from Massachusetts, Malihini calls him "her missionary."

Malihini surfed and fished as a keiki (child), took up hula at seven, performed on a stage for the first time at 12, graduated from Lahainaluna High School, and soon was on her way to a long career in the tourist industry.

Starting in 1993, she served in a variety of posts at KBH before becoming a full-time concierge. Suggesting tours, answering guests' questions and making dinner reservations, Malihini often comes from behind her concierge desk to teach hula on the lawn three days a week. She also hosts a tour of the property in which she explains the medicinal value of various native plants.

Before there was a Ka'anapali Beach Resort, Malihini described Lahaina affectionately as being "nice." Everywhere you went there were familiar faces. When a child was born to that village, everyone was responsible for that child until they grew up. If you got out of hand, because you are on island, your parents knew it even before you got home," she said.

"We were taught to respect everyone of every age." She laments that parents today are not teaching this value. When she sees young people doing something wrong, Malihini turns feisty, getting out of her car to scold kids for not doing the right thing, or asking people to pick up trash they have heedlessly discarded.

One of her biggest passions is hula. She regards it as one of the few things of the past that "we Hawaiians have to hang on to." Learning the words and gestures is incredibly hard, even the first verse, she explained. And then there are six verses.

Malihini is also admired by her KBH colleagues for her remarkable ability to remember the names of previous guests. Many are in frequent email contact with her because of a close relationship with them as they return year after year when she "welcomes them home."

extended family and its kids (the keiki), tutu (grandparents), aunties, uncles, and cousins.
As an ohana, it is common for Kanaka Maoli (native Hawaiians) or locals who have lived here a long time to sing and play music together, dance hula in homes and on special occasions, and sometimes even hanai children in which a newborn is sent off to be raised by

grandmothers and grandfathers as a method of generational bonding.

---
*now retired

THE HOTELKEEPERS:
Mike White And Lori Sablas
The Ka'anapali Beach Hotel
Becoming "the Most Hawaiian Hotel"

SOME YEARS AGO, there was a song, "We are Family" (sung, fam...ii...leee) adopted by the Pittsburgh Pirates baseball team to show cohesiveness. In Hawaiian culture, we have the special word "ohana" for our. There is a special place that embodies the concept of ohana as well as the ALOHA spirit, the love, compassion for others that mainlanders sometimes call the Golden Rule.

The place is the Ka'anapali Beach Hotel (known to locals as KBH), "The Most Hawaiian Hotel." The Ka'anapali Beach ohana is made up of valet parkers and desk clerks, bartenders and housekeepers, office personnel that have bonded with each other in common commitment to spread ALOHA, celebrate the culture and to be "the Most Hawaiian Hotel."

The ohana is also an example of leadership. Its leaders have made a commitment to perpetuate the rich Hawaiian culture that is central to what Maui is all about.

General Manager Mike White and Lori Ululani Sablas* practice the time-honored values that have made Hawaii such a beacon to travelers around the world. Among them are ho'okipa (hospitality), po'okela (excellence) and kokua (helpfulness).

When the special phrase, "The Most Hawaiian Hotel" was bestowed by the Waiaha Foundation, KBH embraced many of 100 different criteria the foundation said should be met by Hawaiian hotels. Sablas, cultural advisor and head of guest services, describes the transformation of KBH from a conventional hotel as fate.

"The stars were aligned," she said. The new Ka'anapali Beach Resort's Sheraton Maui, the first hotel completed in the early 1960s, did not have enough rooms for a scheduled golf tournament. A Las Vegas entrepreneur stepped in and planned and built Ka'anapali Beach Hotel in a record 10 months.

Later, the wife of a Hong Kong businessman Sir Run Run Shaw—a top philanthropist known for his commitment to education—strolled through the lobby, walked to the beach, turned around and thought her husband should buy the hotel. He did, sight unseen.

Run Run was lucky enough to retain Hawaii-born White, a life-long resident with hotel experience and a degree from the University of Hawaii School of Travel Industry Management who has been general manager for more than a quarter century.

White, as Lori tells it, was attending a Honolulu conference at which Hawaii hotel managers were challenged to bring more Hawaiian culture to visitors.

The astute leader listened and began working with University of Hawaii Professor George Kanahele to implement Project Po'okela, a program designed to enhance employees' understanding of the Hawaiian culture and its values so that visitors could have a more enriching and enjoyable visit.

He hired practitioner Akoni Akana, and later Sablas, to be part of a four-person guest services staff that would help turn the hotel into one of the most important educators of visitors in the state.

Sablas got involved after 10 years managing the Ka'anapali Beach Operators Association. An "island girl," Lori went to the old Honokowai School (site of an ABC store today), King Kamehameha III School and Lahainaluna High School. She skipped college because of family finances. "I was taught U.S. and world history but not Hawaiian history. We knew nothing about the culture. Mike White gave me a dream job and the resources to meet the challenge," Sablas explained.

Central to KBH's success are its people of ALOHA. Everyone is required to take a four-hour class on Hawaiian culture on company time developed by Professor Kanahele. Dozens and dozens of classes have been held over the years.

THE ULTIMATE VISITORS:
Chris Marcotte and Gary Bodine
Buckley, Washington
Her Ashes Will Be Here Forever

THEY HANG OUT at the Tiki Bar at the KBH. Meet them and the realization comes quickly that they perfectly represent the passion so many have for Maui. Gary Bodine, a rental specialist who has 15 Maui timeshare weeks that he rents out, and Chris Marcotte, a former massage therapist, frequently listen to some 300 Hawaiian songs Gary has on his iPod on their boat back home in Washington State.

The couple, dividing their time between here and Buckley, Washington, regularly cruise the nearby San Juan Islands. Other boaters think they are nuts playing Iz and George Kahumoku on their boat, but they just smile and pretend they are back on Maui.

In their own words, this is their story.

Chris: "My passion is Maui. I am packed two to three weeks before we come and toss and turn at night because I can't wait."

Gary: "My daughter was very passionate about getting me here, and I thought, you know, maybe there is a reason we really need to come. I didn't have a clue what to expect. We stayed at the Royal Lahaina. It was so beautiful.

"We are avid boaters and fishermen and always have been. We always had loved the ocean. My mom, who is 88, said the family has salt in its veins.

"The first day your head is spinning, but I woke up the next morning and we walked along the grounds and along the beach. All of a sudden, it hit me. When someone said it was a tropical paradise, I knew exactly what they meant."

Chris: "The first night there was a full moon, and we had an ocean front. I stayed up all night watching it come up over the water. It was absolutely beautiful.

"We loved it so much the first time we came; I wanted to cry when we left. We came for nine days and extended for three more.

Normally, we come for a minimum of three weeks and then we extend for a week and then another week.

"And the kids say, 'Are you ever coming home?' And we say, 'Only if we have to.' "

Gary: "We have been coming here for 12 years. It isn't for the pools and it isn't for activities. We take ourselves on trips around the island to Hana, to Haleakala, and learn as much as we can. After a day or so, we literally drift into tropical paralysis — we are so glad to be here.

"When we went to the Big Island, there was a Hawaiian who taught language. She had

Hawaiian letters on a Scrabble board. You had to make a Hawaiian word you knew.

"When you are listening to a song, you don't know what they are singing about. Today, we can look at a street name and know what it means and how to pronounce it. We still don't know much of the language, but what we did learn was that if you look at a word, you know how to pronounce it. "

Chris: "Our favorite things are snorkeling at Black Rock and Honolua Bay, 14-mile marker and at Napili. We go the hula shows. I don't care how many times I've seen them."

Gary: "Today we won't even bother with snorkeling, because we know (the ocean) is churned up.

"Morning is best; we look for the flattest water we can find, because the sediment has already filtered down. I have thousands of photos I have taken underwater."

Chris: "(At home,) I will go on the computer and look at the Napili Kai and Sheraton webcams every day. (That way) I come here every day.

"Out snorkeling, we have pictures of turtles and fish, and I take a lot of pictures of rainbows.

"We go to Hula Grill. We love Moose McGillycuddy's. Typically, we will go to Bubba Gump's a couple times. We really love... Lahaina Pizza Company.

"In Kahana, we go up to Dolly's and Kahana Sands, the little bar there."

Chris isn't here full-time yet, because she also loves the San Juan Islands in the summer. But someday, she will be.

She movingly sums up her passion this way: "I could live here without a doubt. My heart is here. I want my ashes to be spread here — this is where my soul is." If something happens to me on the island, don't take me to home. I will be home." And her ashes will be here forever.

THE BARTENDER:
Dale Simonsen
The Tiki Bar
The 400,000 Mai Tai Man

LITERALLY THOUSANDS know him simply as Dale. Since he made an appearance in my first book about the remarkable people of Maui in 2010, he has been known as the 400,000 mai tai man (he's now made 405,000 over 42 years).*

These days, between mixing mai tais and pouring Bikini Blondes, his many fans often ask him to go to page 81 in "Voices of Maui: Natives and Newcomers" to add his autograph and a "be sure to come back" comment.

More than most people you meet here, Dale is truly a person of ALOHA. For many visitors, first stop after arrival in Ka'anapali is the Tiki Bar in front of an outside courtyard in what is called "The Most Hawaiian Hotel."

The goal is less a drink and more a chance to say hello again to Dale.

Likely as not, if you have been a guest before, Dale will remember and greet you by name thanks to something approaching a photographic memory.

One warm morning picked at random, Debbie and Jim Bruce from the Toronto area—five-time visitors—were at the bar. They presented Dale with a lei to say a goodbye before heading to the airport.

They met the congenial bartender 37 years ago during a delayed honeymoon trip the first year of their marriage, volunteering that their favorite bartender is "the sweetest man," a 'sweetheart," and a special man." Of course, Bruce added, he is an "excellent bartender—very noncommittal in a loving way."

Dale doesn't seem embarrassed to hear accolades. He's heard them many times before.

Another morning Cathy Larson of Stockton, California shows up, announcing to Dale, "we wanted to come down here early because you are so popular." She has been visiting for 20 years. "When we talk about Ka'anapali at home, I find myself telling about Dale, Tommy (Dale's bartending partner of 37 years) and Malihini (the hotel concierge).

"We know you love your job and the celebrity that goes with it," she tells Dale. "It's not easy for two bartenders who work in close quarters to be with each other that long."

Living his first three years in Honolulu, Dale claims to have grown up shy. He had wanted college but family obligations meant he had to go work first as a "mudder" helping preparing grout for tilers at the under-construction Sheraton, then called a hotel, now more grandiosely a resort and spa. Later he took the only other job available: night bellman at the just-finished Ka'anapali Beach. He soon moved to bartending.

Punctuated by his infectious laugh, Dale answers a few basic questions patiently in much the same way he did at the very same bar on a similar morning two years ago.

"I learned on the job (laughs). I had just turned 22 or 23. I never dreamed of being a bartender. I told them I didn't know anything. I was just a beer drinker.

"I had a young style —a different attitude. I worked in the hotel disco in the seventies. We were busy. We didn't have much time to talk to anybody."

His many years at the Tiki Bar have been different. The relaxed atmosphere "allows us to talk to guests more, make 'em feel at home, that they are in a home away from home."

Author: "What makes a good bartender?"

Dale: "Sincerity...efficiency. Be good at what you are doing. If people ask you questions, be up front, be true."

Author: "What do you talk to people about? Do people ask you about where to go?"

Dale: "We talk about family, our kids. When people ask (about restaurants) or where to go, I never answer. They have to find their own things. You learn you can't recommend a place you have never been." (Laughs).

Author: "Have you always been this outgoing?"

Dale: "I used to be shy. Today, I am always talking, having fun." (Maui) "brings out personalities. You develop a little personal relationship with people. Now they are part of me and I am part of them whether they like it or not" (laughs).

Author: "As a bartender, what is your relationship with alcohol?"

Dale: "To me, it is just like pouring water." In the early days, Dale says, he was a drinker. One day when his kids asked to be taken to the beach and he couldn't go because he had been drinking too much; he stopped and has not taken a drink since.

For others, Dale believes in drinking in moderation. He is not above asking someone to leave, however, if they have had too much to drink. "It is my duty to say 'when' you have had enough. I don't do it that often."

Dale's reputation for friendliness is literally known nationwide. Two guests from Wisconsin who have never been to Maui ask the first bartender they see, "Are you Dale?"

Sure enough, it was he. He poured them their first drinks consumed on Maui in two hurricane glasses.

Dale's secret aside from affability is his rule that his bar is like Switzerland. Say anything and his response always will be neutral.

Dale's been there, good times and bad.

When die-hard Boston Red Sox fans saw their heroes on a small TV win their first World Series in 83 years, Dale watched them meet their pledge of jumping fully clothed into the nearby swimming pool upon the sox victory.

On 911, Dale skipped watching the news at home only to arrive to see the towers fall in replay. When the World Trade Center came down, he said, "it was like watching a Bruce Willis film.

"I didn't believe it. Everyone was in awe. It was a shock. All of a sudden we were all subdued; is this happening to us?"

Colleague Tommy Rosenthal, inventor of the lava flow and Ka'anapali float, was asked the secret behind Dale popularity?

Tommy: "He is a kind man,"

Author: "What kind of bartender is he?"

Tommy: "He's the best."

THE CRAFTSMAN:
Mika Villaran
Funny Fabulous Basket Maker

WHEN increasingly famous bartender Dale Simonsen said he made 40 mai tais a week for 40 years, a simple calculation yielded 400,000 of the sweet drinks created over a long career.

Enter basket weaver Mika Villaren, another possible record holder.

Over 20 years, basket weaver Villaren — who also happens to be a very funny man — has made 20,000 coconut palm leaf hats and decorative bowls. (The formula is 40 a week, time-out for six months of vacation each year, times 25 weeks, times 20 years.)

Mika's basket weaving came later in life and sells his creations on the KBH lawn. Tuesdays he teaches ukelele and occasionally can be found trying to play music on the KBH stage. He plays pretty well, but Mika being Mika, this writer never misses a chance to be sarcastic with him.

Asked to talk about his upbringing, he went back to his very first day on Earth, noting he did not remember the doctors and nurses who helped bring him into this Hawaiian world.

Mika's grandfather worked in a pineapple plantation on Lana'i as a luna (boss). Mika's mom worked as a pineapple lab tech for Maui Land & Pine in Kahului. Mika's dad was a mason, mixing mud and carrying bricks in the hot sun to build the old Hilton (now Ka'anapali Villas) and other resorts. Mika wanted no part of masonry.

After boarding school at Lahainaluna High School, the genial weaver by profession reported he was soon eating grits — the kind you get in South Carolina when you join the U.S. Army. After three years of service, as he puts it, "I retired."

Missing home, he came back to enter the tourism industry, working for the old Tropical Rent-A-Car, then driving a tram and entertaining for eight years at Maui Tropical Plantation.

During another eight years at the famous Club Lana'i, the since-closed oasis where visitors were brought to snorkel and ride mountain bikes, Mika was asked to begin making baskets in the Hawaiian tradition.

Today, the newborn weaver sometimes uses scissors to sheer the leaves (ancients used sharp shells to do the same job).

Sitting on a stone-faced low wall at Ka'anapali Beach Hotel four mornings a week, Mika weaves, luring visitors in to watch, sometimes to buy, and more often to listen as he talks story.

Holding long strands of palm, he tells observers, "This is a Hawaiian cockroach. It's a big one. If you run over it on the road, it's like a speed bump. I am not a standup comedian," he volunteers. "I'm a sit-down one." With a few deft twists, he makes an angelfish, offered free to a bystander.

"When you pack it, keep it flat," he advised. "When you get home, push it here. It will pop up. You can use it in a low-maintenance fish bowl."

A lady from Oregon who has come here six years orders a six-inch bowl, which she said she might put bread in. Mika creates it in a few minutes.

"Wrap it in your dirty laundry in your suitcase," he said. Maybe not such a good idea if you are going to put bread in it."

Mika says before starting another hat: "Nice people. People at this hotel like to talk. At other places, they don't," he volunteers.

A visitor from New Jersey and her 13-year-old daughter amble along while her husband and son are off playing golf. Mika extends an invitation. "I've been to New Jersey. Sit down." He quickly asks, "Like to learn how to weave?" Though he rarely teaches, Mika proceeds to teach, handing palm leaves to their outstretched hands.

"Put the leaf in your hand like this. Let the end out like this. Now bring the leaf down and over. Loosen that end up. Leave some space. Poke the other end up. Now, under and over. Bring it around. Now take your other hand and do the same thing," Mika instructs, as the visitors laugh incredulously.

Each of the two made a passable fish. For them, it's off to the beach. "You can go now — it's open," Mika tells them. To round out the day, the weaver will go on to give a ukulele lesson at 1 pm. across the courtyard.

Tomorrow, after more weaving, it will be off to Hula Grill, where Mika will play guitar at a new lunchtime gig.

Although the visitors he meets become instant fans, locals like him, too. A few hours later, Chantelle Crossman, a friend, sums him up: "You know what? He's the sweetest guy." Indeed.

THE CARVER:
Funaki Tupoa
Tap, Tap, Tap and More

TAP-TAP-TAP-TAP... the familiar sound of the Polynesian wood carver invariably attracts a crowd here, as Funaki Tupoa expertly wields one of 20 special chisels and a kiawe wood mallet to fashion turtles, whales tales and tiki warriors that will find a new home on the Mainland. His sales floor is the Ka'anapali Beach Hotel lawn.

Known as Lucky (it is easier for visitors to remember), the powerfully built man who wears size XXXX-L T-shirts and has scars on his right ankle from slips of the chisel who taps away at the Ka'anapali Beach Hotel is one of a half-dozen or more artisans who can be found at resorts and choice locations alongside Whalers Village, The Wharf Cinema Center, Pioneer Inn and Fleetwood's on Front.

The art form may be related to the creation of mysterious Easter Island statues made 25,000 years ago. For years, images of tiki gods (Kane, Ku, Lono and Kanaloa were the principal Hawaiian ones) have been crafted as idols. Tiki sculpture flourished throughout Polynesia for centuries.

A tiki craze hit the Mainland after World War II, when veterans were enticed into places like Kon Tiki Ports in Chicago, with decors that reminded them of their fighting days in the South Pacific. Hawaiians had long fashioned tiki idols to worship.

Tupoa said he does NOT craft idols, because "I am a Christian," a Mormon in fact. My work, he said, is "representative." Biggest sellers are turtles (from the tiny to the large) that go for $30 and up.

The ultimate carving is a four-foot tiki warrior that takes a month-and-a-half to carve and carries a price tag of $3,500.

Most of the Tupoa's customers are Mainlanders. Many return again and again to buy more, because they like his craftsmanship. One couple from Pittsburgh has six and buys another every year.

Tikis patterned after the gods **feature piercing large eyes and mouths with a variety of expressions symbolizing protection, prosperity or other desires.**

Tupoa took up carving 13 years ago

when he was in eighth grade. "I liked to draw, but I wanted to do three dimensional," he explained. The learning began by observing his father and several cousins who were also proficient in the craft.

"The first time you have to sit there and observe. It takes awhile to learn," he explained.

Today a master craftsman, Tupoa acquires tree trunks or large limbs, often getting them from tree trimmers or county work crews who would just as soon have him cut them up and cart them off rather than doing it themselves.

To begin with carving woods like monkey pod, coconut or milo, he strips the bark and cuts the wood to length while Each figure is different. Mass-produced ones often made in China all look alike.

Oahu-born, the son of parents from Tonga who made their living working in hotels here, Tupoa has lived half his life in Lahaina and likes to call himself a Polynesian. (Many carvers have the same Tongan heritage.)

Tupoa carves at home and often works at it 12 hours a day. Three times a week, he goes to the resort. Although he claims to have once been shy, he engages in friendly conversation with visitors who come up as he taps away. "You have to learn to carve and talk at the same time," he noted.

A lady from British Columbia, among the many currently visiting from there, strolls up and picks up a six-inch long wooden turtle with a nice grain.

She thinks she will take it as-is, but then decides the underside should be inscribed with the words "Maui 2013" and the name of the family she will give it to next Christmas. The carver links the family name with the word "ohana," carving in cursive as fast as most people write with a pen.

The visitor wants more. "How about carving the eight Hawaiian Islands on top?" Tupoa takes out a pencil and draws all eight freehand, rendering Maui with a classic bump that represents the West Side.

Is it a good living? "To be honest with you, not really," the carver concludes. Sometimes it's good, sometimes bad," but all in a long day's work."

THE NEW PROPRIETOR:
Bonz Heath
Lahaina Spice Company
Spice it up

LONG-TIME ISLANDS CHEF Gregory (Bonz) Heath and popular concierge Malihini Heath and longtime islands Chef Gregory (Bonz) Heath - two of the nicest people you would ever want to meet - celebrated an anniversary last month. But it was not 11 years of marriage. It was the birth a year ago of Lahaina Spice Company.

The two proprietors formed the mom and pop company to put together love of spices with love of Lahaina. The company's slogan is: "Spice it up."

From Boston, Heath got the Bonz nickname - "everyone in Boston has a nickname" - because he was a skinny culinary worker. Bonz had strong culinary roots. His grandfather was chef on the Queen Mary.

After working his way up in the culinary world in Honolulu and Hawaii Island, he wound up as sous chef at the Ka'anapali Beach Hotel. Bonz and Malihini fell in love (she playfully calls him her missionary because of his New England roots).

While Malihini did her thing (she's beloved

- that's the right word - and one of the most valuable players at the hotel), Bonz moved on to Castaways on the Beach, serving as chef there for six years.

Bonz was always into spices, mixing his own secret blends in a pot for the cooks, discarding what was left over each night. His dream was to own a spice company, a possible path to ending a 30-year culinary career with its 60-hour grueling weeks.

Malihini befriended a couple of guests who happened to own a gourmet spice company. After missing a few visits to Maui because of the down economy, they returned at a perfect time to follow-up on a previous suggestion that Bonz market his spices.

The Bonz-Malihini team set to work. Bonz perfected the spices. For six months, Malihini and Bonz brainstormed ideas on spice names, worked with a graphic designer and ended up with dynamite packaging despite little experience in marketing.

The company's logos include the word "Lahaina" with old-fashioned dialectic marks and an ipu gourd that carries back to older times. Forming the logo's base is a hibiscus, the state flower, all topped by the best over line they could find: Maui no ka 'oi.

The Chef Bonz spice menu features 13 selections, including: Kiawe ("it be smoking") with Cajun seasoning, great for roasting, grilling, braising and poaching fish, or use as a blackening seasoning as well; Kula Garden Blend (Upcountry aromas), "awesome with chicken and vegetables;" Ka'anapali Trades ("a breeze of gusto for chicken, beef and shrimp"); Hawaiian Grill ("grillin' in paradise for all kinds of meat and chicken"); and the top seller, Paniolo Prime Rub (Hawaiian cowboy rub for prime rib, also great for pot roast, London broil and all finer cuts of meat").

The handcrafted gourmet seasons are mixed and packaged on the Mainland by Malihini's spice friend. Back on Maui, the two-person team that started the company without any capital applies the labels.

The company scored a major breakthrough recently, when a Weber grill distributor in Sterling, Illinois, ordered 80 bottles with promise for more.

On Maui, Lahaina Spice Company products can be found at the Ka'anapali Beach Hotel, Maui Prime, 'Aina Gourmet Market at Honua Kai, Maui Gifts in Ma'alaea and VIP Culinary.

At the risk of seeming that this column has

turned into a commercial, it should be said that the original intent was to simply write a small story about a newsworthy company.
But it was clear the tale of these two sweet people simply could not be told in a straight news story.
Today, Lahaina Spice Company is strictly a mom and pop business. If more people want to spice it up, its display spice racks may show up more and more around town.

THE PREACHER:
Laki Pomaikai Ka'ahumanu
Church on the Go
From Green Fields to Saver of Souls

NINE-YEAR-OLD Laki Pomaikai already looked like a loser. Today he may be the most flamboyant, colorful preacher in all of Maui.
His father drank and his family was impoverished. "I watched my father steel a can of Spam. My father literally tied ropes around our house to keep it from collapsing. I was an alcoholic at age nine," he tells his flock of visitors and locals at Sunday services.
The example of his father signaled Laki that stealing was Okay. The future man of God became what he calls "an accomplished

thief" in a pamphlet titled, "From Green Fields Of Marihuana to Prison Greens."

The boy who drank and grew up near St. Theresa Church in Kihei would go on to serve in the jungles of Viet Nam after high school. Returning home, he was arrested in the 80's for growing 800 marijuana plants. He got five years in prison.

Paroled, he later got caught selling cocaine. A judge at the time threw the book at him—a 50-year sentence, minimum 10 years.

And then, a kind of miracle happened. Laki got religion. Behind closed walls 23 out of 24 hours, he had plenty of time to read the Bible, which he now quotes liberally, and knowledgably. His conversion came from within, he said.

Demonstrating his sincerity, he was let go after just 22 months and immediately began religious training at the Cleveland, Tennessee, headquarters of a Pentecostal Christian denomination, the Church of God (seven million members in 170 countries, one million followers in the U.S).

The Pomaikais--like many Hawaiians who form a disproportion share of the population in today's prisons--had fallen a long way. Laki claims he is the great, great grand grandson of

Queen Ka'ahumanu, favorite wife of King Kamehameha the Great.

Laki even adopted a new name: Laki Pomaikai Ka'ahumanu. People in the know say this heritage is true. Following religious training, the Viet Nam veteran has not looked back.

Another place he can be found is near the beaches of Ka'anapali. People learn from his web site, hawaianroyalwedding.com, that they can tie the knot overlooking the beach in a ceremony performed by a descendent of Hawaiian royalty.

A conch shell is blown, a chant given, rings and leis are exchanged and a blessing bestowed.

With Marilyn, his wife of 33 years Pastor Laki has sponsored 21 hanai (adopted) children over a period of decades, taking them in from broken homes, nurturing then and sending them on their way. Many have risen up from nothing like him.

As pastor of Harvest Church on Wainee Street and a church in Lana'i City, Reverend Laki also provided refuge and shelter to battered women, homeless women with children, under privileged and disadvantaged.

Last decade, he also spent two years in Las Vegas ministering there. Today, he preaches at his Church on the Go, holding chapel services each Sunday at 8 a.m. at the Kaʻanapali Beach Hotel.

There he asks visitors to say where they are from and what they are thankful to God for. He plays a religious song on ukulele, and offers stories filled with biblical references.

The reaction to his flamboyant style is positive. Two visitors who heard about him at a luau the night before departure from Maui reported that "we wanted to come here before going to the airport. The luau was wonderful but this was the best part of our trip." Chris Pietzsch, a neighbor of Laki from Kula, allowed that "he speaks from the heart. I have never seen anyone like him. He's genuine." Joe Pluta, a close friend, calls Laki a "Mighty Man of God whose number one priority is to Serve God! He has accomplished many miracles in his life and is a living inspiration." At one service, Laki talks about hell, writes the word on a piece of paper and tears it into pieces after dropping it to the ground. Someone nearby picks it up to take home.

My job is to edify you, build up," he tells visitors. And then he ends with an interpretation of ALOHA.
A. Always
L. Love
O. Over
H. Hate
A. Always.
To that we can say only, Amen.

THE ENTERTAINER:
Alaka'i Paleka
KPOA
Morning Goddess: Missionary Of Music

SHE SAID PIDGIN, the arcane mix of Hawaiian, Portuguese, Chinese and other tongues is her native language just comes naturally, but she can also speak the King's English.

She once wanted to be a missionary in the Philippines. Some years ago, she was christened "Morning Goddess" by a friend, and despite her reluctance, the nickname stuck.

She is Leslyn Mililani Paleka, becoming over 22 years KPOA radio's most popular on-air personality.

Better known by her stage moniker, Alakaʻi, the name for the second in command at hula schools, the morning DJ and frequent master of ceremonies at local events is number one in morning radio and is heard on the Internet by mainlanders who want their Maui fix.

One of Maui's most charismatic characters, Alakaʻi insists the goddess nickname should be with a small "g," as to not to offend the one and only God.

Her philosophy of life is best summed up by her voicemail that begins with her singing "We have been blessed with another day," and ends with "Have a blessed day and know that you are loved."

Aspiring to be a missionary from her school days in Paia, where she was mentored by a Filipino missionary, she said she wanted to go to that country to "save them for Jesus."

My charming wife, when told Ala wanted to be a missionary, quipped, "She may not be a missionary, but she's a missionary of music." How true, since she has mentored many local groups.

Ala has known musicians all her life through her father, Danny "Bully" Paleka, a 100 percent pure Hawaiian who made a living playing piano and operating Maui nightclubs. Musicians were always around; Ala plays the ukulele and a bit of piano.

Danny Paleka met and married his wife (100 percent German) while serving as a Marine in California. She was a student at USC.

Settling in Maui after marriage, they eventually sent their musically inclined daughter to prestigious Kamehameha Schools. There she was enmeshed in Hawaiian culture and its musical tradition.

Ala was encouraged to get a degree in police science at Maui Community College — a mistake, she said.

She did serve a stretch as a parole officer in Hilo, where she had moved earlier with her parents.

Describing herself as a Maui girl, Ala moved back to Maui hoping to get a prison job at the county jail. She ended up fixing up a house she acquired and hanging out for a year when the county showed no interest in a female guard.

Then, at the suggestion of a friend, she applied for a job at the KPOA Lahaina studios. "I started February 5, 1985," she said with precision, and has been with the station all but four years since.

As a DJ doubling as a security officer, she began with an afternoon time slot. Her success secret? Over time, "I had to learn my craft — to be brash. I showed up and I showed well."

Later, she was switched to a weekend show where she grew popular, and finally to a 6 to 10 a.m. program where she has spun records (and later CDs) for the past 17 years. Today she doubles as KPOA program director.

When not on radio, Ala seems to be everywhere as MC at countless festivals and music gigs, two nights a week at Royal Lahaina Luau and at charity events.

Ala is so charismatic with her funny patter and quick quips and jibes at musicians, she often gets equal billing — and, it seems, equal time — with the musicians. Eventually, she lets them play.

Asked where her charisma comes from, she ascribed it to "an appreciation of life," noting, "I have a hale mother and a Hawaiian father. Luckily my brain belongs to my mother. She always thought education was the best gift.

"My father was all about ALOHA. I am fortunate that I have the Hawaiian part. You want to know a lot of different things and be eclectic, but you should always start with love and class and sophistication. That's what I learned from my father."

One of those loves is Maui. "This is one of the few places on Earth people really have a passion for. If you are going to live on Maui, you have to have a passion for it." Right on!

TWO

ALOHA IN KAANAPALI

"Learning the meaning and then living in the spirit of ALOHA by honoring the noblest attributes of our host Hawaiian culture is one of our greatest benefits,"

Realtor Bob Cartwright

THE SERVER:
Christina Olayan
Leilani's on the Beach
Spills, tears, onward and upward

    MAUI GIRL Christina Olayan, age 28, has already been around restaurants and bar food for most of two decades. At six, she bussed tables and gathered up tips at a place where her father—a lifelong bartender—worked. Today, she is a popular server at Leilani's on the Beach.
    As a regular over many years at this popular Ka'anapali restaurant listening to the increasingly popular JD Rocks band on Fridays and Saturdays. sipping Dukes blond, dipping

into an occasional Hula pie, recognizing or getting to know visitors who show up year after year the same month,

watching the passing scene on an adjoining beach path filled with bikini-clad beauties, newcomers in ALOHA shirts, snorkelers and muscular guys carrying surf boards, one wonders what it is like to work in a place like this. We asked.

Once our favorite server Christina would have been called a waitress. No more. At least at TS Restaurants, operator of the highly successful Kimo's and Leilani on theBeach, Hula Grill and Duke's Beach House on Maui, both the women and men who greet and take orders are known as servers.

Christina's work at Leilani's downstairs involves many of the same skills servers perform elsewhere but with a couple of differences. Birds are an occupational hazard and the pace is a lot different than at a typical restaurant, the Maui-born young woman says.

Now and then at the beachfront restaurant a sparrow will zip in. One once swooped through Christina's tray of drinks to fell all the glasses before they reached thirsty patrons. Another time it was a strong wind bringing martini glasses to the floor to shatter on the hard surface.

Most days things go more smoothly. Asked if she ever spills drinks, the young woman proclaims, "*What* are you talking about? I am a professional. I have been doing this for so long I can carry drinks on a tray and not spill a drop unless somebody grabs a drink off it and puts it out of balance."

Another of the things that makes Leilani's different is what she calls "the intensity." Busy as servers at other restaurants are, few are as busy as the ones at `Leilani's` frequented by both visitors and locals.

In a lunchtime shift, a crew of eight servers supported by food runners and people still called bus boys cope with orders for 350 meals. That's more than 40 customers per server.

"We work hard, serving many people at once," Christina reports. Every newbie gets extensive training in every restaurant job before taking a place on the floor. Some don't make it far.

"We had a trainee the first night who accidentally dropped a glass of wine on the head of a small child. He freaked out and ran out of the restaurant not to be found for half an hour." That was his last night.

Some of Christina's server colleagues have been at Leilani's for more than five years. A majority of the restaurant's 49 servers, some of whom work only shorts shifts, have not been around very long. Turnover is high because people work for the quick cash or the experience of working there.

With her good looks, the perky server would appear to be a prime target for visiting guys out for a good time. Christina—who has a boy friend—will have none of this. Her professionalism, she says, keeps being hit on to a minimum.

Only three times in six years have guys made passes at her, albeit half heartedly. Guys sometimes write their phone numbers and names on checks. She didn't think much of the guy one who was with seven male friends especially since she didn't know which of the seven he was.

The name of the game in serving of course is tips. Not as many tip the standard 15 to 20 percent as you would think. The most generous are young people, especially honeymooners. Christina tries hard to build rapport with her customers and succeeds as she is greeted with hugs from visitors who return year after year. "People want memories and I try to create that," she emphasizes. Christina, however, always ranks high in "power ratings" Leilani's keeps, averaging tips of 18 to 20 percent.

To watch the cheerful Christina in action one would never guess that she has had a tough life. Born in Central Maui of Filipino-German parents with a bit of Hawaiian included, she at two-years-old lost her mother—to drugs.

Fighting feelings of abandonment into her early 20's after the divorce, she was well taken care of by her father who ironed, cooked, cleaned and took her camping, fishing and surfing.

At 14 she was shipped off to Oceanside, California to be to with her mother again. Her remarried Mom who still couldn't keep away from drugs promptly confided in her that she was having an affair despite having recently remarried. Christina's step-dad, her second, believed the teenager had lied to him by not revealing the indiscretion and kicked her out of the house.

Such teenage traumas and a soap opera existence left scars. Christina dabbled with alcohol and drugs and became a "cutter." Striving for attention and love, she would slash her wrists. It didn't work. Her mother never asked what the bandages on her wrist were all about. Eventually with the assistance of friends and other relatives, Christina pulled herself together and went on to pay her own way to a small community college to study criminal psychology "because I liked detective stories." She couldn't stand looking at pictures of dead bodies and switched to child psychology, which she may still put to use some day.

Finally seven years ago in California she made a deathbed promise to an aunt to return to Maui to take care of her relative's kids. And here she at last has been able to thrive.

A restaurateur who admired her for her spunk hired her first as a waitress and then to help him start a short-lived restaurant called Blue Moon on Lahaina's Front St. This helped her land the job at Leilanis's where not only customers but also her bosses are her biggest fans.

Christiana's latest setback this summer was the death of her close confidante Carol Coe, the female role model she had long sought. "When I heard she passed, I went into shock.

I rolled up in the fetal position in bed for an hour but no tears came. Just numbness."

Six days later, Saturday afternoon at Leilani's, she looked at the spot where Carol had sat every Saturday and broke into tears. Despite the many challenges, Christina has managed to overcome every obstacle to move to bigger and better things. She says she may stay with the idea of moving up into Leilani's management or someday she just might open her own little café.

Listening to Christina and her rare willingness to open up, one is reminded of the civil rights song, "We Shall Overcome." Christina has overcome.

Now it is her turn to move onward, and upward, as she surely will.

THE CHEF: CJ (Christian Jorgensen)
CJ's Comfort Zone Deli and Diner
Getting Comfortable On Maui

EVERYTHING ABOUT CJ, the Denmark-born Christian Jorgenson, better know as CJ in these parts, borders on the extraordinary. Slim for a chef, 6 ft. 6 inches. Culinary school in Interlaken Switzerland. An early job in a Midwestern suburb, stops as a chef at the

Hilton and Palmer House in Chicago and a prestigious hotel in the former Portuguese colony of Macau on Mainland China, now Lahaina, Maui Hawaii 96761

.For the past 10 years, CJ has been at work 12 hours a day running his own new concept restaurant, Cj's Comfort Zone Deli and Diner. He calls it an upscale fast food restaurant serving "comfort food--comfortable for the stomach and the wallet."

CJ is not at all shy about enthusiastically telling his life story. It includes three pivotal moves that has shaped his life on three continents. CJ begins by noting he was conceived in Iran but brought back to the Copenhagen suburb of Allerod just in time to be born a Danish citizen.

Exposed to good European cooking when small, washing dishes for pay when he was 12, CJ became passionate about food and decided to skip his idea of becoming an engineer. He apprenticed at Copenhagen's most famous restaurant.

Pivotal move number one was signing up for a Danish-American exchange program after culinary school in Switzerland that brought him in 1988 to the U.S. and a position at a Chicago-area Danish American restaurant called Nielsen's.

Next he became at 21 the youngest chef at Hilton for the 2000-room Hilton Hotel and Towers in Chicago. And then a blind date with Marilyn, a hotel management grad from Penn State who worked at the affiliated historic Palmer House. "I was the crazy swinging chef and she was the calm management trainee." They have been married 20 years.

After some years In Macau on the Chinese Mainland where CJ wound up as an executive chef for Hyatt, the couple made pivotal decision number two. Deciding that their two small children should grow up in the U.S. they figured the best place for their kids was neither Macau nor the Mainland U.S. but Maui, with its affinity with Pacific rim cuisine culture they both loved.

CJ the chef presided over a fancy dinner for 5,000 dignitaries the day before the couple departed. Flying into Maui from Honolulu over lush pineapple and cane fields, they quickly knew they were in the right place.

CJ noted that he "did not want to be just another haole (Caucasian) chef who stayed two years and left. We wanted a house. We had a newborn and two year old; after three days we hooked up with a realtor and found a house on the lower road on the beach in a gated community.

We bought a Jeep. You have to have a Jeep on Maui. We put a down payment on a house three weeks after arriving here Starwood after three years made me a corporate complex chef in charge of both the Westin and the old Kapalua Bay Hotel. They sent me to Starwood properties to do assessments. I did a lot of functions in Oahu, Princeville and other places.

After three years, Starwood said they wanted the talented chef who was on a fast promotion track to move to the Mainland. The answer was no. I didn't want to leave Maui My kids liked it; my wife liked it. Pivotal move number three came when "one night I couldn?t sleep." Maui restaurants were expensive, he felt.

There was no place where I could take my little girls and spill on the floor.? And Christian Jorgensen decided to leave and open his own Comfort Zone restaurant

Awakening once in the middle of the night, he mapped plans for and picked a name for CJs Comfort Zone Deli and Diner, a new concept restaurant that would offer comfort good at reasonable prices.

He wanted to offer foods like his grandma used to make but with an international flair. Line two of his business plan was that the restaurant work would provide him enough time to teach his kids soccer.

He and a partner poured half a million dollars into the Fairway Shops business at Ka?ananapli, spending $80,000 alone for a state of the art ventilating system.

"When we first opened we had a bakery but we produced too much dough for two little dough so we shut it down,? CJ says.

"My only home run has been the Hana lunchbox, $12 a person. You get a sandwich of your choice, a quarter of pineapple , bag of Maui chips, a drink and a hana bar, a blend of chocolate and other ingredients CJ won't specify. All come in a returnable cooler. If people call up ahead of time for a lunch to take to Hana, I tell them, 'sir, we don't do preorders. We make it right in front of you. You just come by between seven and eight.' They often buy a cup of coffee and egg croissant sandwich while they are waiting and when they return the cooler all tired at the end of the day, we sell them dinner. So in one day we sell them breakfast lunch and dinner.

Despite inflation, the restaurateur says he has managed to keep the average price of an entree to close to $10 by maintaining a small staff and not using servers or busboys. Customers pick up the gourmet food at the cash register.

The CJs menu includes more than 65 items posted on a colorful blackboard listed in orange chalk top sellers eggs Benedict, coconut prawns, moschiko chicken and mahi mahi, often served with roasted or mashed potatoes or homemade potato salad.

Expanding over the years, CJs also operates a successful catering business that has provided thousands of meals the last eight years for the Hyundai PGA golf tournament in Kapalua and the Maui Invitational Basketball Tournament.

CJ spends about an hour a day sourcing and changing recipes. A sous chef arrives at 5 a.m. to order produce and other perishables. s a top chef, CJ says he has received numerous offers to join elite resorts or restaurants as well as to do TV. He has appeared on the cable TV food network and feels he could have given

Top Chef finalist Sheldon Simeon a run for his money had he chosen to compete as well.

Perhaps it is fitting CJ named his place the Comfort Zone. The master chef from Denmark is as comfortable as can living on Maui. He is comfortable at home too cooking dinner almost every night. He has also made good on line two of his business plan.

"Everybody knows me as the hardest working chef on the West Side. On Saturdays I'd get to the restaurant at four in morning , (later) pick up a couple kids and drive to Kihei for a soccer game, drive to Central Maui for a second game and get in the car and come back to cater a wedding. And I barely missed any practices. (CJ was the coach and he taught wife Marilyn who had never held a soccer ball to coach too.

Though he is proud of the success in he and his Marilyn have built ?she works in the business as well--he is the proudest when people greet him as "Chef."

THE ARCHITECT
Uwe Schulz
Last Stand of an Unsung Hero

THE SIGN ON THE DOOR in the J-Building at the Ka'anapali Royal condominium high above Whalers Village Shopping Center got your immediate attention: "Caution: Oxygen in Use."

It had been more than 50 years since Uwe Schulz, chief onsite architect of at the boutique shopping center that came to be called Whalers Village, landed in California on vacation in 1970, he spoke barely a word of English.

Architect David Carlson Beale, a developer of strip malls, wanted to turn a large swatch of land at the new Ka'anapali Beach Resort into a European-style shopping center. He looked for a European-trained architect to help.

Uwe (pronounced Uva) filled the bill perfectly. Within two weeks of being hired, he was onsite. And he has stayed for the last half century, watching over its design as Whalers Village changed over the years and beginning decades-long service to Lahaina.

He has helped with restoration of the Baldwin Home, orchestrated the restoration of

Hale Pa'i (the "House of Printing" at Lahainaluna High School that produced Maui's first Bibles and grammars in Hawaiian) and been involved in almost every historic building restoration since.

Retelling a funny story on how he happened to land the job in Palos Verdes, California, Schulz told how Beale had gone home to his wife, who was cooking at the time.

"I had the strangest thing happen today. I interviewed this guy who was born in Germany. I couldn't understand what he was saying," Uwe quoted Beale as saying.

"Barbara Beale was a total nut for Mercedes," Uwe explained. "If she drove, it had to be a Mercedes."

She turned around and said, "The Germans built the Mercedes, didn't they?" David apparently bought the argument.

"And that," Uwe said, "is how I got hired."

In the 1960s, Uwe observed, the entire stretch of land from what he calls the Hilton (now Maui Ka'anapali Villas) along today's' beach walk all the way to the Hyatt Regency Maui was empty - useless land unsuitable for growing cane or anything else.

Owner Amfac (now Amfac/JMB Hawaii LLC), operator of Pioneer Mill, offered sugar workers in the 1940s parcels for $2,000 each to build homes. There were no takers. Today the plots are worth millions.

Though a strip mall builder, Beale wanted to build a center that would create shopping in a museum-like setting to celebrate whalers and whaling. And that's what it became - a showplace of low-rise shops, a signature 30-foot skeleton of a whale at the entrance, a whaling boat near the center and a first floor museum complete with whaling artifacts.

The Beales are gone now. The museum is tucked in an upstairs corner, recently stripped of a place to view whaling videos. New owners have also filled the center with freestanding merchant kiosks, some obstructing views of the ocean.

Despite these sad changes, Uwe's overall site design and ambiance remains.

Uwe's biggest contribution, however, may be the preservation of historic Lahaina.

"I came here 40 years ago and saw all these (historic buildings) falling apart," he commented.

Lahaina Restoration Foundation retained Uwe to help save them. One of his most amazing contributions was the challenge of the old Seaman's Hospital up Front Street past the historic district.

One day, sitting in the office of Lahaina Restoration Executive Director Jim Luckey, he told of overhearing a phone conversation Jim was having with a contractor to haul away the remains of the Seaman's Hospital for $2,000.

"It was just rubble. It was a safety hazard for kids, and there was no money to save it." Uwe came to the rescue.

The increasingly prosperous architect decided to take out a $300,000 personal loan from Bank of Hawaii and restore it himself, after the site was acquired from Bishop Museum.

"I put my fortune on the line. The interest back then was 16 percent, but I paid the loan back," Uwe explained.

Uwe went on to explain that he took out a 20-year lease from LRF, which had acquired the site. He moved in his architectural office with six staff members.

It took ten years before he found another tenant, Jim Kartes of the Paradise TV network (another column, another time). Rent from Kartes helped pay back a portion, but not all, of the loan. Uwe repaid the rest and turned the Seaman's Hospital over to the foundation.

The hospital had been built by King Kamehameha III, one of Hawaii's greatest and longest lasting monarchs, as a personal retreat. The structure was constructed from unbelievably strong cut coral as keystones on four corners affixed with fieldstone forming the walls. Old stone, and some new from nearby fields, completed the restoration.

Uwe over the years has also helped restore the Wo Hing Museum, which also had been falling to decay. And when not busy with restoration, he was doing his day job, designing numerous homes ("starkly modern; not appropriate in Hawaii"). This month, he signed on as an advisor for the renovation of Lahaina Public Library.

In the new century, Uwe began battling the big "C." Seeing him at the Rotary Club of Lahaina for a few years, few know his contributions to Lahaina, because he didn't ' talk much about himself.

Few know of his two trips to Egypt, one of the cradles of good architecture, and journeys to Peru, Japan and China, where he sought to learn Asian concepts of buildings that he could bring to Maui.

The world traveler never stopped going after new experiences.

In an act of bravado in his final days, strong-willed Uwe rose from another bed at Maui Memorial Medical Center, got on three planes to Los Angeles; Munich, Germany; and Nairobi, Africa, and went on a three-week safari over rock-strewn roads and muddy terrain.

Harold Hyman of the Rotary Club of Lahaina, a friend, called the trek nothing short of amazing. Uwe rechecked into the hospital almost immediately upon his return.

Next came a wheelchair luncheon visit to the Rotary Club he has belonged to for 40 some years (he is a Paul Harris Fellow for his donations many times over).

And next hospice care at home under medication for pain, sleeping most of the time.

Despite two kidney operations and a half-dozen hospitalizations in Maui, Oahu, California and at the Mayo Clinic in Minnesota, the 69-year-old Uwe never stopped fighting was a fighter.

Hyman earlier had invited his friend to the safari, never dreaming he would come along.

Sure enough, accompanied by another friend, he linked up with Harold and his wife, Vivian - world travelers themselves - in Munich and journeyed to his fourth continent.

There, Uwe delighted in seeing elephants in the wild despite the challenge of failing eyesight. He regaled his companions with stories of trips almost everywhere in Europe to the Great Wall of China, as well as Australian and New Zealand reefs.

Mention anyplace, Harold said, and it would always be, "I scuba dived there." And then there was sailing his own vessel in the race from Vancouver to Maui and road racing someplace lost in the columnist's notes.

Uwe was a quiet sort of man, never boastful of his many achievements. He played a role in helping with the still-unbuilt West Maui Hospital and more recently, despite illness, joined the Rotary Club of Lahaina facelift committee for Lahaina Public Library to interface with the county on tricky permitting challenges.

For whatever reason, friends say, Uwe had never gotten a lot of recognition. He was touched when he was written about in 2011 and kept a clipping posted in his office along with a proclamation of praise from Mayor Alan Arakawa for his work on the hospital. The author was touched, too, when Uwe said, "it was my best Christmas present."

Nine months after that "present," Uwe made his last stand with his first wife Pam and a hospice worker nearby and gently passed away. The historic Lahaina he helped preserve celebrated his life at a crowded Holy Innocents Church where monarchs once worshiped

"You could fill this church many times over with the lives Uwe touched," fellow longtime friend Joe Pluta said in a eulogy.

"The value of what he did is immeasurable. You can't go from one end of Front Street to the other without seeing something Uwe did."

Will Juergen, owner of Saltwater Signs in Lahaina, who migrated with Schulz from California and went along with him to lead a full life in Lahaina, noted that the two attended first grade together in war torn Berlin, Germany, during World War II. "We would play in bomb shelters. You learned quickly to appreciate what you have," Juergen said.

One of the architect's last contributions to the community was helping advise the Lahaina Rotary Club on its restoration permits for Lahaina Public Library.

Uwe's comment at an early Rotary committee meeting that "we've got to do it right" led a decision to remove a tile floor filled with asbestos rather than cover it over.

The gleaming new concrete floor that resulted is one of the most noted features of the remodeled library. He may have been an unsung hero, but he always got things right.

THE CATAMARAN CLAN:
Jim Coon
Trilogy Excursions
Cinnamon Buns and Band of Brothers

THE CINNAMON BUN at one time on Maui reigned as a prime tourist attraction. Read any tourist guide decades ago and you learned of "the famous Coon family" that led snorkel excursions to Lanai'i and served the famous buns on its early morning trips.

Thirty-eight years later, the buns are still leaving ovens as new generations of the Coon family continue to serve visitors. Mama Coon baked for the first 10 years, and her daughters-in-law for the next 20.

Baking is now farmed out. Early promotional material emphasized the family. Today's ads and brochures tout the Trilogy, seen daily on Ka'anapali Beach with visitors braving splashing waves to climb onboard. (Favorite pastime: seeing them sometimes get wet).

Offering some of the most popular catamaran trips in the islands, Trilogy Excursions got its start when Eldon Coon and sons Jim and Rand started building a three-hulled trimaran.

Trilogy was picked as the name to describe the three partners. The story of Trilogy's start is fairly well known (there's a book). However, Trilogy's evolution into a company that has sailed hundreds of thousands of people to Lana'i on snorkel trips to Molokini and sunset cruises off Ka'anapali is not.

The storyteller is Jim Coon, CEO, 66, a modest man whose predecessors go way back to 1888. This—in each generation--is an entrepreneurial version of band of brothers. The first three brothers established one of the earliest holistic health sanitariums in Washington State.

One was also an inventor. Thirty years later, two of the sons of Meade Coon built a charter fishing boat and sailed for Alaska, operating out of Ketchikan and Sitka.

Their charter boat catered to the very rich. One day a visitor who happened to own a yacht once owned by gangster Al Capone suggested that a great destination for a charter boat would be Maui and Lana'i. Eldon Coon knew nothing about the pineapple isle. But he would ask everyone he met whether they had been there and what it was like.

Soon he committed to building the Trilogy with Jim and Rand. The Coons had little funds. So as Jim explains, the father and his two sons spent three years building their dream vessel.

"We worked fourteen hours a day six days a week because we just had sweat equity. We started at 8, took an hour for lunch and an hour for dinner and worked until midnight. We did that for three years."

In 1971, they sailed their 50-foot trimaran (three hulls) to Mexico, Central and South America and even the Galapagos on the way to the South Pacific.

The Trilogy eventually docked in Hawaii, with Jim and Rand falling in love with paradise as well as a couple of island girls. The first Trilogy excursion to Lanai was launched on July 5, 1973.

Lana'i Island then, as now, was privately owned. Others had tried to start a Lana'i trip but never asked permission. The Coons became the first to ask for an OK, agreeing to restrict tours to weekdays so locals could enjoy their only beach near Lana'i City without have it besieged with tourists. The Coons won landing rights, which they have enjoyed ever since.

Six passengers paying $35 each made the first trip. Jim and Rand captained. Trilogy was on its way to becoming one of the most popular visitor adventures on Maui.

The original Coon family—the third generation is now active in the business—couldn't have imagined six different Trilogy catamarans would bring what easily could be hundreds of thousands of visitors in more than 10,000 trips (estimated) to a beautiful snorkeling beach on Lana'i.

While a lot about Trilogy has been the same, change has been no stranger either. Captains Jim and Captain Rand, as he is known, would land on the Lana'i' beach and fire up a huge wok.

The captains were the cooks for the midday feast, and today's captains still are. The Coons rarely captain this days but Chris Walsh still does. He's been captaining Trilogy I through VI for 33 years.

Trilogy VI now makes the 90-minute run, along with Trilogy I (new ships sometimes take on old names). Frolicking dolphins still frequently greet visitors as they near the Lana'i port but the harbor itself has gotten a major facelift, looking a lot better than Lahaina Harbor.

Trilogy Excursions added a snorkeling trip to Molikini in the mid-1980s as well as popular sunset cruises from Ka'anapali. Navigation is now by state of the art GPS as well as radar.

Fifteen years ago the Trilogy Beach Activity Center opened at the Ka'anapali Beach Hotel. The center dispenses towels, offers snorkeling, scuba and snuba (scuba equipment attached to a tether) and was the first on the beach to give paddleboard lessons.

Trilogy guests line up in front of the shop to hop aboard, sometimes getting wet in the process. If waves are too big for a safe departure, guests are ferried to Lahaina for boarding there.

The Coon family entrepreneurship tradition lives on in Randy's son Riley is a captain; Denver teaches snuba and works on the boat and Lilly is in-group sales. Jim's daughter, Ginger, manages the activity shop; Lianne handles PR and marketing.

Though personnel may have changed, one thing never does: the cinnamon buns.

THE REALTOR:
Bob Cartwright
Whalers Realty, Inc.
Provider Of Dreams Does More Than Sell

Affable, astute Bob Cartwright, co-owner with wife Tess of Whalers Realty Inc., the largest independent real estate firm on the West Side, has been around long enough on Maui to be a strong believer in ALOHA. Asked about his experience with hundreds of visitors, the former Chart House cook who transferred from California years ago volunteered this about his clients:

"I've watched people's health improve when they move here. There are five top benefits: better health, learning ALOHA, enjoying natural beauty, pursuing of the intellectual and spiritual, and the happiness of owning a home in paradise.

"Research has shown that due to our weather and lifestyle, people live longer and happier lives on Maui than anywhere else on earth.

"Learning the meaning and then living in the spirit of ALOHA by honoring the noblest attributes of our host Hawaiian culture is one of our greatest benefits," he said.

Cartwright, like a number of successful businessman started as a waiter here. , He has become the most influential and successful real estate broker on Maui.

In the business of helping people enjoy the benefits of Maui, as he puts it, the hardworking Cartwright has been watching and participating in the mostly ups — and sometimes downs — of West Side real estate from his headquarters at Whalers Village over three decades.

Transitioning into real estate from the restaurant business, Cartwright secured a real estate license when a partner at Whalers Realty recognized his potential and offered to bankroll a real estate licensing course for him.

Cartwright joined the company he and his wife Tess would one day acquire in 1983. His start with Whalers began in the office of Jack Kelley, one of Whalers Realty's four partners. A short but sweet hiring interview went this way, Bob reported:

Kelley: "I hear you want to work for us, and I like the fact that you have a track record representing developers on new projects. I hear you are pretty good. I think you could make a contribution. But let me tell you how it works around here. If you ever come into my office and ask me a question, you are fired."

Cartwright: "I'm a big boy. I think I can handle that."

Kelley: "Well, get the hell out of here. You're hired."

In 1981, Bob had met Tess Hallmark, an artist, on a cruise ship off Hawaii Island. He was there on business, and she was drawing caricatures, dabbling in real estate and looking for someone to dance with.

The two joined Whalers Realty together and began running ads using the phrase, "Ask for the Best," patterned after the Biblical phrase "ask and thou shalt receive" to distinguish themselves from other agents.

Kelley, in ill health, later sold them the firm in 1993. Soon, "Ask for the Best" became the slogan of the entire company and applied to all of its agents, who now gather to shout it out in TV commercials.

Fast growth brought Whalers Realty from six agents in the early 1980s to 35 at the peak under the Cartwright's' ownership and sales of at least $100 million a year. Agents during this tougher market now number 24.

For one of his clients, Cartwright has bought and sold whopping 25 purchases — some transitional, some for investment.

The most pleasurable achievement for Maui brokers, he said, is helping people realize the benefits of living on Maui.

The Cartwrights have seen it all: years when 12 percent interest was considered normal, times of difficult markets in 1982 and 1992 and frenzied times of skyrocketing prices, when almost everything quickly sold.

Mellowing after years in the business, riding the peaks and valleys as real estate soared or collapsed, Cartwright's philosophy is that what Realtors do is not so much sell real estate but help people with transitions in their lives.

It starts with what this principal broker calls "the thrill of helping the first-time buyer." It then moves on to helping find a larger home when a new baby arrives and finally putting a retired couple into a retirement dream home. Or, in less pleasant circumstances in between, helping a relocated divorcee.

"There is also the ability every day to appreciate and enjoy nature, and the ability to grow and mature through a plethora of opportunities available through community groups and organizations.

"And finally the happiness that springs from the security of owning a home in this beautiful and special place," he added.

THE AUTHOR
Norm Bezane
Ka'anapali Kids for 27 years

MAINLANDERS often fondly remember summers at the lake. Our family waxes nostalgic about decades of vacationing on Maui before we, as parents, became permanent residents in 2001.

This reminisce, taking a look back at the ever- changing Maui seen as experienced from a visitor's perspective, offers a glimpse of how Maui has changed, and how, in some respects, it remains the same.

Thirty years ago, when the world famous Ka'anapali Beach Resort was a one-time dream destination for legions of bubbly honeymooners and visitors on seven-day package tours, those with that first time in paradise glow didn't think much about coming back.

Our kids were an exception, returning on vacation with us nearly 27 different years in the seventies, eighties and nineties.

They stepped foot on Maui for the first time on Hawaiian Airlines planes that then debarked people right on the tarmac before there were jet ways. Over the years they rode in "umbrella" strollers, toddled across rope bridges, sailed on catamarans and floated over Ka'anapali on a parasail, as they grew older, finally returning as adults.

These days' visitors arrive at fairly cosmopolitan Kahului Airport. In those early years, you hopped on Hawaiian Air on Oahu after a trip from the mainland and deplaned to walk to a sleepy baggage claim area, picking up your bags near a tall tree that stood in the center of the terminal.

Today, from our bulging photo album, spring forth not only of our "Ka'anapali Kids" but the remarkable evolution of one of the world's best-planned and workable resorts—a resort that no longer is the exclusive paradise for just newlyweds and first time tourists. Now, as the ads say, "the world comes to play" and Ka'anapali Kids once so rare can now can be found on every beach and around every corner, many on return trips.

Paging through the family album not only brings back memories of the seventies, eighties and nineties on Ka'anapali: it brings the realization that we have more photos of our kids two-week sojourns to Ka'anapali (often each Easter) than from the 50 weeks we spent annually at home in Chicago.

And there are even some from Honolulu, including one memorable frame taken when an entertainer we remember as "Sonia" picked our baby up and sang to her at the old Garden Bar at Hilton Hawaiian Village.

The first night away from home of our six-month-old daughter was spent at the Kahana Sunset even before there was a Kapalua just up the road. Evenings were enjoyed in Ka'anapali or Lahaina, with our daughter frequently tucked in a stroller sleeping under a restaurant table somewhere while we dined on ahi or filet mignon.

Given our daughter's continuing ability to fall asleep easily anywhere, we used to say that our young traveler had slept at all the best restaurants in Lahaina, including Kimo's and even outside the fancier Longhi's Restaurant, parked on the sidewalk below an open window. We dined just inside to the amusement —in those days—of not so-frequent passersby

Though we are still lean people, a lot of the photos and memories revolve around eating. At our usual 5 a.m. jet-lagged awakening on a first day in Maui, we evolved a tradition of driving to the Hyatt (then called a hotel and not a resort) for an early walk through the Japanese garden.

Pineapple pancakes in LahainaTown at historic Pioneer Inn overlooking the harbor would follow this. Once or twice a trip we would return, broiling our own dinners you could cook yourself in the interior courtyard (mahi, seven minutes).

The cook-your-own barbecue pit is no more, as are most of the hundreds of whaling artifacts on the wall of the bar within view of a fleet of fishing boats. Now only a few remain.

The broil your own concept was also a staple at the Old Rusty Harpoon, since reinvented as the only true sports bar on Ka'anapali Beach, now recently moved to a new location near the entrance to Ka'anapali (another change.

We'd grill our own burgers--some of the best we've ever tasted--against a backdrop of fresh sea air and Moloka'i in the distance. Another favorite spot was the old Crab Catcher restaurant, predecessor to today's popular Hula Grill at Whalers Village Shopping Center, centerpiece of the resort area right on the ocean.

Besides scrumptious nachos unlike any to be found today—so it seems—the Crab Catcher featured a small swimming pool where our kids could wade or swim while we ate hamburgers (we both still ate meat and had better teeth in those days).

Also remembered fondly was the nearby Chico's, *the* place for tacos before anyone had ever heard of one of today's island favorites, Maui Tacos. It was at Whalers Village that I once left our newborn son in a stroller in the aisle of the old bookstore next to Rusty Harpoon, only to leave and then remember that we had had a second child and he had been left behind. (He was still there, fast asleep alongside the Hawaiana book section).

And then there were daily visits to Yami Yogurt for a product so good we wished we could get it in Chicago and nearby Ricco's, the cozy open air pizza place where a "new" air conditioned fast food court now stands. Both have been casualties of progress.

Our Ka'anapali Kids did more than eat and stay on the beach. We'd go to the community Easter egg hunt under the Banyan Tree in town each year, with our son one time finding the golden egg entitling him to special prize, a canister of Play Doh. And of course there was

Easter egg coloring at three different resorts and the Makawao Rodeo on Fourth of July.

There were family milestones too. One life-changing event occurred on the curving golf course lined pathway along Ka'anapali Parkway one evening in 1981. My wife Sara and I made a life-changing decision that one of us would quit work.

In the days when it was rare for husband and wife to both have demanding careers with two kids, it was along Ka'anapali Parkway that I decided to quit my job as a corporate publications manager and stay home as one of the earliest househusbands. Today, passing by now almost daily, I remember the walkway fondly since the decision there, it turned out, was one of the most rewarding ones I have ever made.

One blustery day on our 23rd trip, tragedy almost struck. In a first and only use of a video camera, I decided to film an entire day of our favorite family activities, mynas chirping at wakeup, breakfast at Pioneer Inn, a ride on the Ka'anapali resort trolley and a day at the beach.

Videotaping away, I was glad to see the enormous and picturesque waves that wife and kids plunged into for "the ocean shot." Problem was my wife got in trouble, saved only by the fact that our daughter had become a good swimmer. Our 34-year old refuses to look at the video to this day. Our Ka'anapali Kids are no longer kids now but they still keep coming back from Chicago and New York to what we sometimes called "Conorpali Beach. We used to say to our young son Conor that one day he would own one of the houses behind the colorful rows of azaleas facing Honoapi'ilani Highway in front of Ka'anapali Beach Resort.

He doesn't own one yet but you never know. But his Ka'anapali parents now own a permanent residence close by up the hill from Ka'anapali not far away. Since 2001, we've learned that living on Maui is far different than visiting.

We came from a big city, and this is a small town. One of us—not me—thought we'd get "island fever," a fear that a small island would not be enough to keep us happy and busy. Alas, we have found that music is everywhere, almost every weekend brings a festival and the days are so packed with work or community related activities visits to the beach become rarer and rarer.

Years ago, in the Midwest, family memories of many people used to revolve around summers at the lake. Ours are filled with fond memories of Ka'anapali Beach and Lahaina, as they will in the years ahead for increasing numbers of Ka'anapali Kids building new traditions on the greatest place on earth. Maybe some will even up here living here, becoming voices of Maui too.

THE MASCOT
Kea Aloha
Day in the Ka'anpali Life

AS THE ONLY NATIVE HAWAIIAN in his family, born in Hilo, weaned in Honolulu on Sand Island, arriving on Maui via Hawaiian Air just three months after birth, Kea Aloha loves living in Ka'**anapali.** Mostly he is pretty silent but sometimes he speaks up. The white fluffy guy frequently petted by visitors who miss their animals' love is a dog.

The vet has said he has a very strong heart. That's because his co-masters walk him down and then up Keka'a Drive hill every morning to visit the resorts and sit on a soon-to-be-rented beach cabana chair to watch

Trilogy snorkel day-trippers depart each morning. Kea spends more time at the beach than many residents, who mostly seem to go to and fro to the store or other places unconnected to the joys of paradise. Kea takes up his story in his own words.

Kea Aloha volunteered at Lahaina Public Library with co-master Sara Foley during the Rotary Club of Lahaina?s modernization project.

"My first stop in the morning is the Kaanapali Beach Hotel valet stand, where I say hello to my friends Patti, Bobbie, Clayton and Ron (who keeps insisting I need training).

I go there so often I have become a bit of a mascot. Bobbie calls me Mr. White which makes two of us there. The taller Mr. White is General Manager of the hotel

"To let other dogs know I have been around, I raise my hind leg on my favorite signs - one saying 'Stop' and another, 'No Parking. Your Car Will Be Towed by Alii Towing.

"'The ocean used to scare me to death - even the sound of it before I could see. Now it merely frightens me.

"Back home, I like to sleep around. Favorite spots are a doggy bed next to an open window, sofa, lounge chair and cold marble in the bathroom.

"I go to a lot of places, particularly liking

the Sunday Drive to Ulupalakua Ranch, where I once heard Amy Haniali'i sing at the winery. I had to stand outside the white picket fence, though.

"My co-masters like to order elk burgers at the ranch store. I have been to Whale Day in Kihei and heard Neil Abercrombie and Alan Arakawa speak at the Maui Tropical Plantation before they won election.

"I don't like politics, though - tired of my masters watching 'Morning Joe' on Tivo and the 'Last Word with Lawrence O'Donnell' on MSNBC. My friend Tommy thinks I am a conservative, but as usual. 100 percent of the time he is wrong. I don't like Fox either. since I do not like animal channels that put out false 'information.'

"My favorite hangout place is Paia Fish Market, where I sit under a picnic table and watch the masters eat ono fish sandwiches that they claim are the best on the island.

"Must they always eat three times a day? When little, I once took a dump on the threshold of the Paia bikini store, where my of my co-masters likes to sit watching women try on bikinis.

"I have been on vacation to Chicago, but the last trip was harrowing. American Airlines was fine without a reservation. But on a second trip on United flying out of Honolulu, a clerk asked for my reservation, and I had none. We missed our flight, and the co-master had to take me in a cab outside the airport to a freight building and wait six hours for another flight.

"In the evening, I sometimes go for a run with my friend, Parker, a tiny dog who recently broke his leg jumping off a sofa and had to have a metal plate put in. No more incessant ball chasing for him.

"I also sometimes blitz at home around the kitchen counter, the dining table and sofa when the co-master decides to chase me. I could be a great NFL halfback because of my quick moves, since the co-master never catches me. A football is too big for me to carry, however.

"I have become famous, though. I am pictured on the Lahaina Library Facelift Timeline blog, because I served as a volunteer for the Rotary Club of Lahaina modernization project. And I have been praised in a book for not eating the author's manuscript for breakfast.

"Bedtime is around 10. Sometimes the co-master falls asleep on the sofa watching

'House,' and I have to bark to get her to join me in bed with my stuffed pig, the love of my life, who squeaks when I put her in my mouth.

"'So that's all, folks,' as a famous woodpecker used to say. A hui hou and be kind to anyone with four legs. See you at the beach, but not close to the water."

THREE

ALOHA IN LAHAINA

"She put away her server outfit and was named "Miss ALOHA."

Ron LaClergue
Kimo's General Manager

THE HOSTESS:
Laura Blears
Kimo's Restaurant
From Famous Surfer To Hostess With The Mostest

SHE WAS THE FIRST WOMAN in the world to win money in a surfing contest. She posed surfing for national magazine leaving little to the imagination. Her illustrious father, Lord James Blears — his real name, not a title — advised her to "go for it."

She was a Smirnoff vodka girl, posing in a white swimsuit on a surfboard for a promotional poster sent to every bar in the islands. She appeared for three straight years on ABC's "Wide World of Sports," "Challenge of the Sexes" as well as it's

"Superstars," competing with the likes of NFL football star Dick Butkus and others.

She appeared on "What's My Line," a popular network show in the 1960s, whose panel members had to guess the profession of guests. Nobody figured out she was a world-class surfer.

She is Lahaina's Laura Blears, formerly Laura Blears Chin and Laura Blears Cohn, who has been the "hostess with the mostest" at Kimo's on Front Street for the last 10 of her 29 years there.

"We were trained that you go out with your hands full and in with your hands full," she explained. The years there have flown by because she loves it so much, she said. Eventually, her wrists gave out with carpal tunnel syndrome.

By now, she believes, she would have been in management if she had not damaged her wrists.

"Managers work very hard. They bus tables, bring out dinners, carry the ice buckets along with their management duties," she added. Though Laura completed half of a 100-point training program, she gave it up knowing that her wrists would not handle the strain.

About a decade ago, she put away her server outfit and was named by then-General Manager Ron LaClergue as "Miss ALOHA," assigned to rove around tables and chat with diners. She was so good at it; she was moved to the hostess stand, where she has been ever since. Despite the fact that she is over 60, once a surfer, almost always a surfer.

"When I was growing up in Waikiki it was a magical place," she noted. "As a little girl, I used to surf against the boys, because there were no girl surfers." When not on boards, Laura, before she was ten, paddled in canoes and rode on catamarans.

"My dad brought us over here in the early '50s. We lived right next to the Duke's statue on Waikiki Beach."

Kalakaua Avenue — now a tony shopping area with a beach (it used to be a beach with some shopping) — "was a two-way street. We were in the old Judge Steiner's building. It had the very first surf shop in Hawaii underneath. Its owner was a friend and moviemaker. He made "Slippery When Wet," one of the first surf movies," Laura said.

"We started surfing when we were little kids. All the beach boys took us out. (Years later), I took my son, Dylan, on a surfboard before he was a year old. We surfed every day.

"The beach boys would take us surfing all the way out to the break. We would stand up with them — even did tandem surfing on top of their shoulders while the man is surfing on the wave. I competed in that when I was 14 years old.

"My father became a surfing champion. He surfed in competitions. We all surfed in competitions; it was just a way of life. My dad would say, 'You feel like doing something and it is fun, let's go to do it!' Encouraged to surf by her father, Lord James Blears, known to beach boys as Tally Ho, Laura entered her first competition at 12. She lost. To seek comfort, she remembers running to a beach towel shack and crying.

The famous seamstress there was named Take (pronounced Ta-Kay). She used to make all the surfers shorts. No other surf company made them to order.

"I ended up being asked by surfing legend Fred Hemmings to enter my very first contest for money. My brother was a finalist in that very first pro contest," she recalled.

Laura was an alternate, but the next year she was a real participant.
"It was billed as '325 men and Laura.' That was the advertising. I beat one guy in my heat, but I never advanced. And I never ended up on the circuit," she said. Against women, however, she had at least ten wins.

Thirty-two years ago, surfing in Waikiki mostly gave way to parenting, working and surfing on Maui after she moved here with her first husband, Bonn Chin.

A while later she joined Kimo's as a cocktail waitress, just five years after the now-famous restaurant opened.

Laura's surfing today is a bit more limited. She still surfs when she can between hosting at Kimo's, teaching water aerobics

THE PARROT MAN:
Brian Botka
PURRFECT Days in Paradise

IN THIS ERA of the digital camera—clunky version, hand held, I-phone or I-pad—no visitor or resident no matter how many sunsets, hula dancers, rainbow or plumeria photographed this or in past years is ever going to beat out Brian Botka.

The job of the "parrot man of Front Street" Wednesday through Sunday evenings is bringing joy and a permanent record in the form of a photographs of people with parrots to thousands of customers. For 20 years Brian has happily worked for a company originally formed three decades ago by one Bud "the Birdman" Clifton.

Brian is much more than a casual clicker of a camera. An artist and accomplished photographer in his own right, the parrot man selects from five multi-colored parrots, micas and cockatoos that he perches on hands and shoulders of customers. On go silk leis just the right color to match what customers are wearing. Brian snaps away, finally proclaiming, "PURRFECT."

Listen in as he talks to both birds and customers, his usual street patter beginning with, "Come on up. They won't poop on you on my shift–guaranteed."

Brian, to a new customer: "Hey ...hold my little baby, lay 'em down. Now what I am going to do is a few different shots. We will put Mai Tai (the youngest parrot at 14) on you. He is not going to guber on you.

"Don't show fear, people; they sense fear. Now I am going to put a bird on your head.

He wants to be top dog today. Oh this is going to be beautiful. I want that chin forward," he tells a lady on the left.

To the bird Mai Tai: "Preen her hair, make her look good," Botka watches the parrot gently grab thin strands of his customer's hair. "Good boy."

To the customer: "Don't worry about a thing. You are looking good."

To the bird Mai Tai: "Mai Tai, look at the camera. Peanut, look at the camera, man. On one, two three...." (Click).

To the customers: "That's excellent. Stay with me. I want to see your teeth. This is a photo you will want to see forever. Awesome. One two, two-and-a–half, three, big smile... This is a phenomenal shot. Got it. PURRFECT, excellent job, very well done."

Typically Brian puts birds on a tiny baby, a three-year-old with a toothy smile, and a parade of family groups, among them he said "one poor guy" who was here with six older sisters.

Over the years at the parrots' perch near the corner of Pioneer Inn facing the public library, Brian's film and digital camera lenses have captured everyone from celebrities to a group of two dozen cheerleaders all in one frame here for a contest at the Hyatt.

Actor Dustin Hoffman one time brought back from Lahaina a parrot picture and added a painting from artist Jim Kingwell for good measure.

Carlos Santana and his new wife have been in. So have movie stars Demi Moore, Danny Devito, Arnold Schwarzenegger and even President Bill Clinton's political consultant James "it's the economy, stupid" Carville.

A bit of a political junkie himself –his brother works in Washington—Brian engaged Carville in a memorable four-hour marathon conversation right on Front Street. He also got a hug from Mary Matalin, the "raging Cajun's" conservative wife, who he said was the sweetest, smartest person he had met for a long time.

Joking with clients in ways that bring automatic smiles, Brian says purrfect so often when he looks through the lens that one bird, noted it well. One day, in parrot speak; he spontaneously began crying out "PURRFECT" all day. Tiring quickly of the gambit, the parrot hasn't returned to using the word since.

Brian is quick to point out that parrots are one of the oldest creatures on earth.

"They are telepathic and very intelligent," he says. "They work on a higher frequency and notice things I would never notice. Birds know enough not to eat all the fruit on a tree. Humans will and later they will starve. "

The birds are purchased from breeders. Though he often kisses them on the beak, he has never been bitten though he has had parrot fever.

In the early days, he used film—so much that that a photo store set up a branch right in Pioneer Inn to process photos overnight ($60,000 worth of prints a year).

Today he used a $2000 digital camera that converts his shots to mega pixels. Costly laser printers then turn out a purrfect product. The results from the photographer and the printer continue to be "PURRFECT" every time.

PRESERVATIONIST: Jim Luckey
Lahaina Restoration Foundation
A Luckey Lahaina Tale

LIKE THOUSANDS of other visitors before and since, Oregon sawmill salesman Jim Luckey and his wife, Annie, fell in love with

Maui on their very first visit and thought they might like to live here.

The Luckeys wasted no time, moving to Napili a couple of years later to start a new career.

Picked over 23 other candidates, Luckey succeeded Larry Windley to become the second director of the pioneering Lahaina Restoration Foundation in 1973.

The next 26 years, he shepherded through the preservation and restoration of irreplaceable sites, including Hale Pa'i (House of Printing), the seamen's cemetery alongside Maria Lanakila Church, the steep-walled Old Lahaina Prison, Seamen's Hospital and the Wo Hing Temple, a meeting hall built by Chinese immigrants

His pride and joy was Hale Pa'i built in 1837 at Lahainaluna High School. The fieldstone for the structure was carried high up the hill to Lahainaluna Seminary by students. "They certainly didn't go up there with a Caterpillar truck. The stone got up there on someone's back," Luckey observed

When the restoration began, birds were roosting in the 125-year-old rafters. There was a hole in the roof, and the place was falling apart.

The restoration team replaced 23 sets of decaying window frames, fixed the interior and added a new shingle roof with the same number of rows of wood as when it was new.

Maui Community College's Industrial Arts Department built a 600-pound working replica of the original press used to print grammars and Bibles in Hawaiian, and Luckey had it carried by brute strength into the refurnished white structure. Artifacts and displays were added before the opening in 1981.

Luckey early on put Lahaina in the forefront of a national restoration movement, roving Eastern U.S. historical sites for ideas and pioneering the concept of adaptive use. He knew that not every building could be turned into a museum.

The Seamen's Hospital became the office of architect Uwe Schulz, who played a key role in its restoration. Later Jim Kartes' Paradise Television Network, the Visitor Channel, moved in, paying an annual rent and filling TV screens with Lahaina history.

Had it not been for farsighted leaders who created two historic districts more than 50 years ago, there might be no restored treasures, Luckey points out.

At the beginning, in 1959, there was Keith Tester, general manager of Pioneer Mill Co. Later joining in was Carolina-born Larry Windley, a charismatic diver and victim of the bends who ended up flat on his back with nothing to do but read.

Windley spent three years at the Children's Missionary Society in Honolulu researching the town's post missionary history and become the first executive director of the Lahaina Restoration Foundation.

Windley's partners in early restoration efforts included employees of the former "Big Five" company Amfac (later acquired by JMB Realty, Chicago). Insightful county officials and master craftsmen took steps to put little Lahaina on the map as one of the first towns outside New England and Virginia to embrace historic preservation.

As Jim tells it in a very fine book, "Luckey Come Lahaina," people like Tester and his wife, Frances, were driven by love of Lahaina.

"The sugar people feared that the vast development in store for Ka'anapali in the

'60s and beyond would overwhelm Lahaina and destroy the beloved town as they knew it.

Fred Baldwin, descendent of missionary Dwight and Charlotte Baldwin, weighed in early by donating a quarter-block site containing the Baldwin Home and the Masters' Reading Room, where whaling captains once hung out.

Blaine Cliver, an architect appropriately from New England, where Lahaina's missionaries sailed from, drew up restoration plans for the home. He hired George Wylie, a master carpenter, to put his skills to work restoring not only the home but also Hale Pa'i.

The Baldwin Home was stripped to its bare stone two feet deep. The interior of the home was duplicated right down to replicated wallpaper. The historic landmark on Front Street opened in 1966.

Luckey, Windley's successor who is now retired in Eugene, Oregon, ran a very progressive Lahaina Restoration Foundation from 1962 to 1987. Successors, Keoki Freeland and Theo Morrison have since restored the iconic Pioneer Mill Smokestack, symbol of the town.

Morrison more recently has launched many more initiatives that celebrate not only the missionaries but thousands of plantation camp workers who populated the town most of the last century.

Luckey, executive director emeritus, is now in a well-deserved retirement. What he does now in his mid-80s is "go fish as much as I can. No, I didn't do much fishing while in Lahaina." He had no time.

THE MERCHANT:
Jim Killett
Lahaina Galleries
Artful Journey

AS THE ART CAPITAL of the Pacific, Lahaina boasts more galleries per capita than almost anywhere. Had it not been for a lot of rain in Germany back in the 1970s, things might have been different.

Jim Killett, former small college football player, football coach in Okinawa of all places, ex-marine, along with wife Nancy, once a gymnastics coach, wanted to travel the world,

Killett, a self admitted conservative sort who started saving for retirement right out of school decided to take a risk and pour all of the Killett's life savings into a business. "It took guts to quit my job," Killett noted but it rained a lot in Germany where he worked.

The future entrepreneur took to watching a lot of TV, especially the hit show Hawaii Five O. Killett fell in love with Hawaii and knowing he could move anywhere, chose Maui.

Landing in Wailuku with no job, he stopped by a real estate agent who was advertising for a salesman but found by a twist of fate he was out to lunch. Killett then drove to Lahaina, saw the harbor, and knew he did not want to live anywhere else.

An ice cream parlor and an art gallery were for sale but the ice cream shop was taken off the market. So Jim ended up calling Nancy back in Arkansas to proclaim: "We just bought an art gallery."

Jim knew nothing about art. "Lahaina Galleries had one painting for sale by David Lee, sold art prints, and even puka shells.

In the early days, Jim used to ride his bicycle along Front Street with the gallery open. When a customer entered, he'd hop off the bike.

Three decades later, Lahaina Galleries is one of the most successful businesses in the state with galleries in Lahaina, Wailea, and on Hawaii Island, and Newport Beach.

Lahaina Galleries today represents 20 or so international artists, many who live, paint or sculpt in Maui. Three were born in Italy, one in France, one in Argentina.

How did the former football and gymnastics teachers do it?

Apparently with a lot of luck, good ideas, honest operating methods (some art dealers have been known for their crass selling methods), relying on good people and adding artists who had to meet one important criteria (they had to be masters of art technique).

In the 1970s, the Killetts signed on two budding stars, Paris-born Guy Buffet, known for the whimsical scenes of old Hawaii and Paris bistros, and Robert Lynn Nelson.

Lahaina Galleries was one of the earliest promoters of marine art, nurturing Nelson's career until he moved on with Jim's blessing to establish his own gallery. Buffet is still with Killett after all these years.

Lahaina Galleries has spawned many imitators, propelling Lahainatown from a place with only two or three places selling art to more than 21 galleries today.

Another key move, initiated by Jim and Joan McKelvey the Lahainatown Action Committee years ago was the start of Friday Night is Art Night in which galleries host some of their artists and offer visitors pupus and wine.

Lahaina Galleries artists make up a true ohana, with artists even dropping in on art night even when they are not even scheduled to appear.

You can no longer find puka shells at Lahaina Galleries. Serigraphs start at $500. The most expensive art: $500,000 for the work of the late renowned sculptor Frederick Hart who has one of his pieces at the site of the Viet Nam Memorial in Washington D.C.

Today Nancy Killett, vice president who has been involved in the business from the beginning, after raising sons Beau and Lee, the gallery's web master, has a second passion beyond the gallery: she teaches Sunday school and is the very busy head of the Lahaina Baptist Church Youth Group.

These have been and continue to be sunny days for the Killetts on Maui with a few clouds added during more difficult economic times but those rainy days in Germany are long past. There are no more puka shells in the gallery and Lahaina averages only 12 inches a rain a year.

THE ARTIST:
Jim Kingwell
Kingwell Island Art
Painting The Town Red, Green, Yellow and Blue

PROLIFIC ARTIST and good soul Jim Kingwell has set up his easel alongside Lahaina sidewalks to lure in customers during Friday Night Art Night for years. By his estimate, he has easily painted 3,000 original works of art, many featuring Lahaina Town landmarks.

Through this Oakland, California-born oil painter and watercolorist, hundreds of visitors have brought a piece of Maui back home — scenes like crowds in front of Cheeseburger in Paradise or ocean view landscapes.

. Celebrities like TV sports legend John Madden, Dustin Hoffman (also photographed by the Parrot Man), Donald Trump, Olympian Dorothy Hamill, Arnold Schwarzenegger and art aficionados around the world display his work, often created plein air (painted outdoors) in Hawaii, Finland, Switzerland, Chile... even Easter Island.

Kingwell, son of an airline mechanic and grandson of a Finnish masseuse — both his grandparents and father came from Finland — was inspired to paint by a third grade teacher.

From California, "we started flying to Hawaii on those four-engine prop planes in 1955 when I was five years old," as he tells it. "We could come on a dime because of the employee discount, and we did that once every other year until I was 14.

"I always had an inclination to draw. I remember drawing on little paper bags in Yosemite," he recalled. After one Hawaii trip, his teacher asked him to draw on the class chalkboard.

"I drew a palm tree, a hula girl and Diamond Head. It stayed up there for a week. That was a real plus for a kid," he said. This was that moment Kingwell realized he wanted to be an artist.

The would-be artist kept drawing all through grammar school and high school. During high school, "I won a summer scholarship at the San Francisco Art Academy. My folks were ecstatic," he recalled. Later, the college-level program extended a full scholarship.

He trained with practicing professional artists — "It was a great school." Among his teachers was a famous courtroom sketch artist who had drawn the notorious killer Charles Manson in jail.

After six years in the Air Force and reserves, he turned to painting to make a living, traveling the world. After a failed marriage, he returned in 1989 to Hawaii, "a very healing place" he said.

"I had forgotten how great the weather was, being able to paint outdoors every day."

"I knew diddly about running a gallery," he confessed. Kingwell's success is rooted in his ability to create representational art, a romanticized realism that he embellishes with a touch of whimsy.

"I like to capture the initial attraction of a scene that has light or colors I like. A lot of people say my work makes them feel happy. That's good. There's enough negative" in the world, he said.

About half of his work is landscapes; the other half what he calls "building art." He has painted hundreds of structures, filling them with colorful characters. The artist has filled hundreds of sketchbooks with drawings of people, many made at airports, which he uses to populate his painting.

Will the prolific artist ever run out of subjects in Lahaina? "No way," he is quick to point out. "There is always something different. Lahaina is changing, too. I almost think I am a historian at times. I paint something that you think is going to be there forever, and it disappears."

Does he have a love affair with Lahaina? I guess so, he smiles. "It's a pretty nice spot."

THE POP ARTIST:
Davo
From Hippydom to Pop Artist

LOOKING LIKE an early '70s-style hippie ("I was a real hippy, not a pseudo one"), hanging out once with Bob Dylan and Joan Baez in Huntington Beach, California; now well-dressed, still equipped with long wavy blonde hair, pop artist Davo has had the kind of life movies are made of. And as a celebrity name-dropper on Maui, he has no superior.

Davo thinks women are the superior beings on the planet and credits (count 'em) about a half-dozen of them with all he is or has become.

The special women after his mother include Barbara Pyle, who got him to New York; mentor and founder of the Lahaina Arts Society Alexandra Morrow; and Lynn Shue of Village Galleries, who first displayed his art in a fancy setting.

Davo's life is storybook. Born in Los Angeles in 1950...grew up five miles from Disneyland and surfed in Southern California.

He gardened for Ansel Adams, the iconic western photographer at Big Sur ("I learned a lot from him").

To avoid the jungles of Vietnam he substituted what he calls the jungles of Kauai, where he wore next to nothing. Then it was on to Tahiti, where he mostly played and occasionally painted badly, he says.

His idyllic and hippie life lived with all its accompanying habits ended one day when he hurt his back surfing. Needing rehab, one of the earliest of the influential "Davo women" sent him to her home in New York, launching a major life change. There he met pop artist Andy Warhol.

Since he was a kid, Davo reported, "I wanted to be a painter. My mother encouraged me. There were always crayons and watercolors around." After meeting Adams, he wanted for a time to be a photographer.

By the time he reached New York, he'd gone through cubist, Gauganesque and Daliesque periods. The name dropping Davo's penchant for friending celebrities got him an invitation to visit Warhol's famous studio, the Factory.

"Andy took a liking to me. Though he was very busy, he let me hang out," Davo said. He observed the artist's pop art technique of beginning with a photograph and turning it into a painting.

The dirt-poor Davo saw the chance to combine both of his interests and actually produce something that would sell.

The choice for his first subject? Sex symbol Marilyn Monroe, based on a photo in a newspaper. Warhol's parting words to him when he headed back to the islands were "that would be a great start."

The technique involves making a stencil-like silkscreen of a photograph. A kaleidoscope of paint is daubed on a canvas. Expensive, powerful lights burn the image on the canvas, and embellishments with the brush transform the photo into a work of art.

As Davo tells it, he took his last 100 bucks and had a silkscreen of the Monroe image made by a T-shirt maker. He would use it until it became threadbare.

Back on Maui, with no money to buy expensive lighting equipment, he adopted the nearest best thing: Maui's incredible sunlight. At high noon to this day, he burns images onto canvases with 25-second exposures.

Since 1983, Davo has taken Warhol's method a step further. He mixes phosphorous with acrylic and coats the canvas.

Customers in effect get two pieces of art for the price of one. Turn out the lights, and his paintings glow with a quite different look.

"At first I thought this was gimmicky, but art is anything that moves you. I finally realized there was nothing wrong with that," he said.

On Maui, Davo's uncanny luck continued with a humorous twist. After ten years at the Banyan, Shue came up to him under the tree, said she liked his art and way with people and wanted to bring him into a new gallery.

"Just then she turned around, and a bird made a big dump on one of my paintings. I was thinking, 'I am out of here.'" A lady walked up, loved the painting, thought the "paint" was still fresh and bought it on the spot. She never knew what made it fresh.

The starving artist days are long gone, with his work sold in both the Gallery 505 operated by another key woman in his life, Belinda Leigh, and Village Galleries.

Three weeks after Davo moved to 505, an executive with the Grammy Awards showed up, saw his painting of the Beatles and said the artist could get tickets to the prestigious award dinner if he would donate $10,000 worth of art.

Davo figured that would be four paintings. He's been attending for ten years, has a vote in the competition and was thrilled recently "to have dinner" with Paul McCartney. The legendary Beatle had a table in front, Davo, in back.

Davo's women have played such a crucial role in his career; you'd think most of his paintings would be females. Not so. His favorite subjects have been the Beatles, Rolling Stones and Einstein, of all people.

"All the women in my life have been so marvelous, and the men can go to hell.
"But," he was quick to add, "not you, Norm."

RENAISSANCE MAN:
George Kahumoku
A Grammy Award Winner Lights A Fire

DOING MANY of the things that Hawaiians have traditionally done, including fish, farm and play music, multiple Grammy Award winner George Kahumoku Jr. has had a life full of choices.

He could have been a successful artist or a prolific farmer, or a teacher who could use his skills in art to boost the confidence of troubled high school students, or an itinerant player of music, or a big name entertainer.

As a matter of fact, for a while, he was all of these, all at the same time.

Always reinventing himself between struggles to make ends meet, after a bout with cancer at age 27, the energetic and genial Kahumoku, now 60, normally gets only three hours of sleep each 24 hours – a good thing, considering his many interests

Precocious even at four, a keiki who loved to sketch horses on his parent's farm, George won his first scholarship to attend classes at the Honolulu Academy of Art in 1954. More scholarships followed to Kamehameha

Schools and then the prestigious Rhode Island School of Design.

He skipped Rhode Island for a full scholarship at the California College of Arts and Crafts in Oakland because it was closer to home. The talented artist, trained as a sculptor, ended up after graduation teaching art to kids in the inner city.

He turned them off putting graffiti on walls and onto to painting giant murals on downtown buildings with permission of an enlightened landowner. City officials were so impressed with this son of Hawaii that they made him art commissioner for California's Alameda County, including Berkeley. Then opportunity knocked twice.

Kamehameha Schools wanted him back in Honolulu to teach art. The job fell through, but he got a reprieve with an offer to start and become principal of a new Kamehameha Schools facility on Hawaii Island near the legendary City of Refuge.

Struggling to make ends meet, he enthusiastically signed on. Ever restless, however, that, too, yielded to still another lifestyle.

Kahumoku started a farm on Hawaii to raise 1,200 pigs a year. This he found was a quick way to go broke, which he did. In 1990, George began playing slack key guitar at the Mauna Kea Beach Hotel. Management insisted George perform with a partner. To keep it in the family, he picked his son, Keoki. Hands shaking, playing poorly, Keoki barely made it through the first set, supplementing his poor playing with an even worse voice. No worries.

"At the break," George wrote, "I grabbed Keoki's ukulele, used my wire cutters and clipped each of the strings on his instrument. From a distance, you couldn't see they were not connected."

The two "played" like that for months, musician and pantomime in perfect harmony. (Despite the rough start, Keoki today is a slack key master and Grammy winner).

Uncle George (the tag "uncle" is often attached to locals because so many are related to one another) finally figured out the best way to make a living was to play music at the venues along Ka'anapali and eventually settled in Lahaina.

In 1992, George began playing at The Westin Maui, with one memorable, funny result that had nothing to do with music.

Living at the hotel, in an ultimate clash of cultures, Kahumoku and Hawaiian friends one afternoon decided they had enough of restaurant food. They would revert to their Hawaiian ways, grab nets and go fishing at Pu'u Keka'a, known to legions of visiting snorkelers as Black Rock.

Bringing along handfuls of peas, like those used by visitors to attract fish, Kahumoku and friends cast their nets and pulled in a mother lode of uhu (parrot fish), manini (sturgeon), aholehole, u'u and others.

Figuring they should avoid cleaning their catch at The Westin's spacious pool, they returned to their room, filled up the bathtub with fish for cleaning and flushed the entrails down a single toilet until it clogged up.

The fish would have to be dried. They strung up ropes, lined them with fish and turned on the air conditioning. Odors of drying fish wafted through the entire floor — the fishermen didn't realize the AC vents circulated air from one room to another.

Time to cook: gather dried kiawe wood stacked outside the Villa Restaurant. Find some rocks around the waterfall. Group the rocks into a small roasting pit on the fourth floor lana'i, and lay a wire shelf from the minibar across the rocks. Fire it up — barbecue a huge kala fish on the open fire. Then walk down the beach for a Hawaiian supper.

The sirens of fire engines are not often heard along Ka'anapali Parkway, but they were that day. Yellow-coated firemen strung up a long ladder to the room to put out the tiny flames amid the rocks, blasting a big hole in the sliding glass door with the powerful stream. Another day in paradise.

The story is told in "A Hawaiian Life," the self-published book George sells at his slack key performances. Such mischief has been a way of life for a man whose infectious laugh is duplicated only by his wife, Nancy, the sister of his first music publisher.

By the 1990s, George was playing 15-20 gigs on Maui a week and traveling to the mainland, playing at performing arts centers as far away as Carnegie Hall in New York. Then, with a flash of insight, George adopted a new approach that sent him on the path to winning Grammies.

Why not duplicate on Maui the successful concerts George appeared in on the mainland? Stage your own weekly concert series and charge admission.

Paul Konwiser, a retired computer whiz with NASA and big fan, put together the first show. Clifford Nae'ole, the able cultural practitioner at the Ritz-Carlton, Kapalua, offered an auditorium. The Masters of the Hawaiian Slack Key Guitar Concert Series was born.

Years later, George and as many as 20 guest artists a year are still going strong, recently completing well over 300 performances at the Ritz and a new venue, Napili Kai Beach Resort.

Dancing Cat Records came calling a few years ago. Impresario George Winston regarded George's "melodies and his voice as a gentle Hawaiian breeze."

That breeze, plus the slack key music of a dozen others the last few years, has brought three Grammies and a recent nomination for a possible fourth based on weekly appearances by George and a dozen or more artists, including Uncle Richard Ho'opi'i and up-and-coming Peter deAquino.

Standing alongside his favorite goat near lush rows of taro and sweet potatoes, farmer, teacher, award-winning musician and composer George Kahumoku Jr. reflected on a versatile life. "My music makes the most money, teaching makes the second most money, and the farm always loses all the money," he said. But life to George isn't about money; it's about farming and giving back.

Six years ago, George also became a "weekend farmer," building a new home on a 4.5-acre plot near Kahakuloa on the North Shore. In Hawaiian tradition, sustainable agriculture is a community way of life.

George and scores of volunteers, including residents, his students and even Mainland visitors invited up for the day, have turned four acres of scrub into a cornucopia of agricultural riches.

There are 80 varieties of taro, 3,000 pounds of sweet potatoes in the ground, and 30 varieties of citrus. A man favoring superlatives, George claims to have 100,000 plants.

Much of the output is given away, although taro for poi is sold at modest prices to his Kanaka Maoli brothers and sisters at ten distribution points around the island.

Back home, munching a succulent give-a-way papaya from his farm, popping a slack key album called "Drenched in Music" in the CD player, a writer struggles to fashion a last good sentence about this amazing man. In essence, George is a Hawaiian and a man of ALOHA in the best sense of both words.

THE ENTREPRENEUR:
Michael Moore
Old Lahaina Luau
Bringing Authentic Hula to Hundreds of Thousands

CHANCES ARE GOOD that when a visitor asks a local about the best luau, the answer will come back, "Old Lahaina Luau." Though all others are enjoyable and fun, Old Lahaina to many stands in a class by itself in quality and contributions to the community.

Old Lahaina Luau dancers have performed before tens of thousands on the islands and literally millions on TV during the annual Thanksgiving Day Macy's Parade in New York City and on ESPN during half time shows at the annual Maui Invitational Basketball Tournament.

Talk story with lead partner Michael Moore, and it is quickly apparent that this culturally significant, enormously popular Lahaina based enterprise represents perhaps one of Maui's most successful homegrown businesses created since Maui became home to resorts.

In fact, it now is a multimillion-dollar company that employs a third more people than Maui Land & Pineapple Co. when it was a fairly sizable enterprise.

Fortune magazine each year lists the most admired and best companies to work for. It is no exaggeration to say that the company named Hoalohs Na Eha (meaning four friends) might just make one of the lists.

The luau's long journey began almost 25 years ago when Oregon-born Michael Moore and accountant Robert Aguiar were working for the Ocean Activity Center. Management of the 505 Front Street center suggested the tourist company start a luau.

Moore, then a sales representative, was intrigued, thinking it would be nice to be an evening bartender there. Moore was used to steering visitors to luaus. "I told people luaus were kind of corny; the food is not that great, but you are in Hawaii so do it."

Three months after the luau opened, Ocean Center backed out, thinking the luau "did not have much potential." Moore, Aguiar, Kevin Butler and Tim Moore thought otherwise. They raised funds and birthed what has become the most authentic luau in the islands.

No fire dancing either, for this would be a true Hawaiian luau. (Fire dancing is a Polynesian tradition but not Hawaiian).

Not everyone was impressed. In the early years after its founding along the shoreline at 505 Front Street, a Honolulu critic called it the worst luau in the islands. In typical Oahu-is-the-center-of-the universe fashion, the critic claimed the best one was at Waikiki's Royal Hawaiian Hotel.

He said that luau on Oahu was best because you could sip a great cabernet with a view of Diamond Head — a measuring stick of dubious merit, Moore noted.

"At first, the review pretty much devastated us. We really loved what we were doing, and it was a lot of fun. After a few days of being distressed, we said, 'Let's take this review as a template for change to the luau.' We added flower leis, upgraded all the food — we really looked at every aspect of what we did, including the way we greeted people. We made it more Hawaiian and personal," Moore said.

"We felt there was a need to present Hawaiian music in a really respectful way that honored the culture — that didn't make fun of it.

"People were making fun of poi. Poi is a staple of the Hawaiian diet. You cannot make fun of poi."

What Hoaloha Na Eha did over the years, as Moore puts it, was "raise the bar of what a luau could be. These were mostly hotel functions. We visited every commercial luau in the state. We wanted to create something that honored the culture. We did that very well for 12 years at 505 Front Street," he continued.

"And then we wanted to build an outdoor culture theater. HoALOHA Na Eha added a new venue ocean side from Lahaina Cannery Mall. The spacious grounds provided for a place for culture demonstrations before the feast and hula show."

HoALOHA Na Eha was also lucky to acquire a kitchen at an adjoining pizza restaurant that had closed. There it could prepare luau meals featuring Hawaiian and American fare. The company also opened ALOHA Mixed Plate, which quickly became a popular gathering spot for locals.

Nearly 25 years after the start of a luau "that didn't have much potential," Old Lahaina Luau welcomes 400 guests a night, seven days a the week during peak tourist times, some 10,000 guests a month.

That adds up to lots of leis, mai tais, and even plenty of poi served on the nightly buffet. And quite a bit of joy too.

THE KUMU (TEACHER):
Keali'i Reichel
Learning Hula: a Passion to Perform

SINGER, SONG WRITER and Kumu Hula Keali'i Reichel, a son of Lahaina, is nothing short of amazing. He's won 31 Na Hoku Hanohano music awards, Hawaii's version of the Grammys, including four as Hawaii's top male vocalist. As a kumu hula (hula teacher), he brought his halau to the Merrie Monarch Festival for two straight years and won top awards against stiff competition.

As a strong supporter of things Hawaiian, Reichel is a founding director of the Hawaiian immersion language school that is working wonders preserving the Hawaiian language. Reichel recently decided to enrich the lives of would-be dancers, both experienced and newbies, by teaching the keiki, kane/wahine and kupuna in three separate Saturday classes that run a tiring total of five-and-a-half hours.

The kumu began the first classes by telling students that hula has to become their obsession. Students were taught that to enter the halau they would need to learn a chant they would give at the beginning of each session. "Our ancestors did not have doorbells," he said.

One of the first days Kumu instructed his dancers on the beginning grounding position. He also noted that he is always to be addressed as Kumu.

"Everything starts from here with flat feet," said Kumu, pointing to the ground. "Feet flat, toes touching each other, shoulders and body relaxed, arms extended. You don't take big steps. You will lose control of your body if you do. Check the position of your feet.

"Use your extended arm to bring yourself around. You need to control your body from the tips of your toes. That is the name of the game – control.

"Up and down, up and down. Polish this step all week. After five or six weeks you will be precise. You must practice this every single day. Point your hands with precision. Check the position of your elbows. Bring your hands up to form a flower.

"When I tell you to freeze, you should have such control over your body that you keep your feet together. I may sound like a broken record. But you have to go all the way down to look nice."

Over the months the students fully embraced Kumu's disciplined approach and found as they learned that his 30 years experience teaching hula was already paying dividends.

We love it but it takes a lot of work was their universal comment. They indicated that the authentic hula, absorbing the inner meaning of mele and chants of authentic hula, brought their knowledge of the culture to another level.

Learning the language in order to interpret the dances properly is tough. "The keiki absorb the Hawaiian language like a sponge," a student noted. "When you are older, you are still a sponge but the water drips out fast."

Practicing the grounding position, repeated again and again and accompanied by a chant, takes all morning. In the weeks ahead, the na haumana (students) will learn all the basic movements.

Watching hula over the years, one never ceases to be amazed at its beauty and grace, the intricate movements and the ability of each dancer to remember every motion from hands, hips and feet above, below and beyond.

Learning hula is a journey of a lifetime. When asked how long the new classes for West Side residents would last, Kumu's response was quick: "Forever."

THE OLD TIMER:
Sammy Kadotani
OK, OK, the Man Who Can't Say No

IF YOU LIKE THE WORD "OK," you will love Sammy Kadotani. The 91-year-old community treasure who was described years ago as a "perpetual motion machine" in this newspaper is persistent in using the word "OK" all the time. As a matter of fact, he is persistent in everything, whether it's buying a house or asking for a contribution for his latest cause.

In his distinctive talk story way, Sammy described his first adventure with home ownership.

SAMMY: "There was this house they were building — a sample home. I said, 'What the hell, I have to start looking for a home.' I fell in love with that. It was right on Wainee Street further down from the Catholic church.

"Finally, I came home and said, 'OK, I made up my mind; we are going to buy that house.' It was a three-bedroom. The wife asked, 'Where are we going get the money??' I was working at the Pioneer Mill office for $250 a month. That is OK. I will try to go to the bank. The banker was Jack Vockrodt.'

The conversation, according to Sammy, went like this:

BANKER: "OK, Sammy, come on it. You want to buy a house? How much does it cost?"

SAMMY: "$9,600."

BANKER: "OK, come back tomorrow."

SAMMY: "So I went back, and I sat down."

BANKER: "I want all your expenses. Do you drink?" "Yeah. I drink." "How are you going to pay me? You do not have enough."

SAMMY: "I will never forget this: fifty-seven dollars and 72 cents a month (would be the payment)."

BANKER: "OK, you come back tomorrow."

SAMMY: "I must have gone back to see him about 15 times. And he never gave me that answer... finally, the contractor said, 'Sammy, are you going to buy the house? I have to paint the house.'"

SAMMY: "So I said, 'OK. I will try one more time.' So I went down to the bank."

BANKER: "You tell him wait to paint. You come back tomorrow."

Disgusted, Sammy told the banker he would take his business elsewhere.

BANKER: "OK, OK. I will approve that."

SAMMY: "And then I had to borrow $2,000 from my mother. I paid her off slowly, and it took 15 years. When Raymond, my son, finished Lahainaluna, the loan was paid off."

In the early days, Sammy had a chance to take over his father's fish store on Front Street. He wanted no part of it, since as a kid, he could be found usually chopping fish rather than playing baseball. Instead, he became a timekeeper for the mill, showing a talent for management. One if his six bosses once suggested he take a job running the Hotel Hana, but he declined.

His next assignment was to manage Pioneer Hospital, run by the mill. When the hospital closed, doctors formed the Maui Medical Group. Sammy came along to run that. And when Kaiser Permanente came in to build a clinic, Sammy moved over there to run that for 13 years, too.

Sammy's other talent has been raising money for every conceivable cause. His mind for dates may not be what it once was, but he remembers every project and every idea he put into action.

He pushed to get Lahaina a community swimming pool, raised money for a $15,000 electronic scoreboard for Lahainaluna High School, and in 1987, he ran a Lahaina community reunion that attracted 3,000 people.

In 1994, he formed the PGA (Proud Grandparents Association) to raise funds for King Kamehameha III grammar school. He recently decided that it should have a statue of the great king to commemorate the school's 100th birthday. He signed on a sculptor and raised $5,000 to help pay for it.

Lahaina Restoration Foundation needed to sell bricks to finance the restoration of the Pioneer Mill Co. Smokestack. With Sammy in charge, LRF has sold more than 1,000.

An avid golfer, Sammy played at Ka'anapali in the 1960s for $12 a round. He quit golf because it became too expensive, but not before playing in "Swinging with Sammy," a golf tournament for locals he organized that continued for 20 years.

No profile of Sammy is complete without mentioning boats. With friends, he used to remove the metal from old plantation house roofs to make tin boats to ride out to the waves. The kids used washboards as surfboards.

His front yard features a canoe once used in the Spencer Tracy film "The Devil at Four O' Clock," which was filmed in Lahaina. Painted on the side is "E komo mai" (welcome).

Among Sammy's proudest achievements and highlights of a long life was his first trip to the Mainland, bringing along 21 Boy Scouts to a national Jamboree in Colorado and traveling for six weeks by plane, train, automobile and bus.

Pride in his sons and grandsons is also a highlight. The Kadotanis put two sons through college. Raymond runs Take Home Maui, the "pineapple store" on Dickenson Street, and Owen worked for years as a chef at Ka'anapali resorts before opening a business.

A grandson is about to graduate from law school, and a granddaughter works in human relations for Hula Grill.

Sammy's favorite relaxation may be watching the San Francisco 49ers. A fanatic, he tapes all the games and watches them again and again. He still can't get over last month's Super Bowl loss and "the terrible call by a referee.

"I've watched it three times. And they lose every time!"

Over the years, his wife, Hatsumi, has tried to get him to go to the beach more. "But he just can't stop," Sammy said.

He summed up his own life best: "I like to help. People say, 'Hey Sammy.' I can't tell them no. When do you want me?"

THE CULTURAL ICON:
Charles Ka'upu
1957 to 2011
A Special Moment: the Passing of a Legend

ON A BEAUTIFUL late August Saturday morning in 2011, with waves pleasantly lapping to announce their arrival on the shore, a slight breeze wafting through, catamarans bobbing gently in the ocean, Maui and Hawaii commemorated in memorable manner a man who has done as much as anyone to celebrate Hawaiian culture.

Charles Kauai Ka'upu Jr. — a giant of a man in more ways than one—was a revered cultural practitioner, master chanter, former cook and master of ceremonies for 22 years at Old Lahaina Luau.

One of the founders of the Celebration of the Arts at the Ritz-Carlton, Kapalua, one-time KPOA disc jockey known as "Bushman," Charles as a kumu hula mentored dancers on Maui, Kauai and Japan.

At the Ritz celebration of Hawaiian culture, one of my first conversations with this imposing, large man years ago began with this question and a gesture to the heart: "Why would a guy from Chicago feel so passionate about Maui? Where does this come from?"

"Well," Charles noted, "you have probably, in another life, been here once before." A pleasant thought I have never forgotten.

On this Saturday, the majesty and spirituality of Hawaiians — and the feelings of those of us who admire Hawaiian culture but come from other places — was eloquently evident as we all sat or stood in silence, except for frequent chants in a broiling sun for 150 minutes as the tributes came forth.

Kupuna, Charles' sisters, friends and workers all stepped to the Old Lahaina Luau stage in groups and individually to chant or come forward in silence to offer up hoʻokupu.

Some 129 people by actual count, including Hawaiian brothers with shaved heads and bodies (a show of respect), some dressed in black with red others in white or green, brought up ceremonial gifts in the form of chants or intricately woven forms of lei as a tribute and sign of respect.

Saturday evening, the people who knew him best and some who simply admired him came to celebrate a life that was full of teaching the culture.

Hokulani Holt of the Maui Arts & Cultural Center, said her close friend was always ready to teach the culture, to share. He taught the various hotels in Ka'anapali and Wailea what it really means to be part of this land, the ocean, and all that envelops us, she said.

Maui Visitors Bureau head Keil'i Brown, who made many Mainland trips with Charles to bring the Hawaiian cultural story to local travel writers, remembered when he heard of his passing that — strangely — he smiled and was actually happy.

In a previous near-death experience, Brown related, Charles had been to the other side. He was ready, and he said he was ready.

Afflicted with asthma that sometimes took his breath away, Charles was no stranger to calling 911. He did so unsuccessfully for the last time on July 12, 2011.

In a laugh-filled eulogy, his sister, Keʻala, recalled Charles the boy who always had to be cleaned up for. Those who knew him, Keʻala said, would know cleaning up for him was a horrendous task.

As an adult, Charles loved to cook, but he used every pot in the kitchen, she reported. Though quick-witted with a strong sense of humor to the point where tears would run down his face, Charles was better known for his serious side. He wanted to teach where Hawaiians came from and would say the breath of the culture was in its language.

Charles loved hula, kahiko, the ancient kind, but Holt pointed out that he had a grand time doing ʻauana (modern) as well.

Charles last words on his Facebook page were, "I am." Today he rests at peace in Kaʻopala Bay.

FOUR

ISLAND HERITAGE

"At night, they feasted and the girls danced the lascivious hula-hula."

Mark Twain
Author/Humorist

IN THIS SMALL BOOK, *by necessity, we learn about only a few of the contemporary people who shape today's island life.*

Many more are among the missing, left to interview and write about at some future date. The number of remarkable people encountered every day by a writer who gets around a bit seems inexhaustible.

One of the biggest shapers of these islands—King Kamehameha the Great—brought Hawaii together as one. And one of the best representations of the culture—the mystic of ancient and modern hula danced in homes, community gatherings and at resorts— is an everyday reminder of the heritage of these islands.

The tales that follow don't quite fit the theme of this book but nevertheless represent my continuing quest to know more about how Maui became Maui.

THE KING: Kamehameha I
Kingdom of Hawaii
Warrior, Unifier, Surfer, Trader
Shaper of Maui

KING KAMEHAMEHA I, first of an early line of kings, was trained to be a fierce warrior. Some 200 years ago, the powerfully built, square-jawed warrior completed the unification of the Hawaiian Islands after conquering Oahu, Maui, Lanai'i and Moloka'i.

When locals think of Kamehameha, we think of King Kamehameha III Elementary School named after his son, Kamehameha Avenue in Kahului, the famous Kamehameha Schools and even the official Kamehameha Day state holiday in June.

Few remember that a nuclear submarine was named for this Hawaiian, and that his statue is in a place of honor in the U.S. Capitol at Statuary Hall.

Kamehameha did not cut down a cherry tree, nor did he wear wooden false teeth, yet he could be considered the George Washington of these islands.

If alive today, the great king would probably lash out at the comparison, since he was a great fan of Great Britain, a country he considered a protector of the islands.

His exploits are richly described in dozens of books by numerous illustrious historians—Lahaina's David Malo included.

Kamehameha was born of ali'i (kingly) lineage on Hawaii Island. He had the physique of a tall, muscular NBA player.

Some believe the future monarch was born in 1758 at about the time of Haley's Comet, an event mentioned in prophecies as signaling the birth of a powerful king.

The fledgling king already had mega mana (a word meaning acquired authority, power and prestige) derived from two royal parents who each had considerable mana in their own right.

Mana was acquired by inheritance or heroics in battle. Battles were often fought to acquire more mana.

Tradition says Kamehameha got even more mana when he acquired the hair of the slain Captain Cook, explorer of the Pacific Rim. Hawaiians believed Cook also had a lot of mana.

The remains of the man who named these Sandwich Islands were treated in the traditional manner after his death on the beach near Kona. The flesh was deboned and the bones wrapped in kapa (tapa) cloth in such a way that no sound could enter. The bones were then hidden.

Kamehameha, an admirer of Cook, had visited his ships, although that had nothing to do with the explorer's demise.

Kamehameha fought his first battle on Maui at 17 in an unsuccessful effort by a Hawaiian ali'i (king) to conquer the island.

Later, after moving a 5,000-pound stone called Naha which legend said could be moved only by a man of destiny, the powerfully built warrior with the fierce face set forth on his life work of conquest.

Wars were declared by cutting down a coconut tree in another's territory. Battles were fought according to rituals, traditions and rules. Kamehameha was no stranger to either.

To invade Oahu, in a feat of organization, Kamehameha assembled 36,000 warriors transported in 800 canoes. (Kamehameha organized his units in groups of 400. Thus, he marshaled 900 sets of troops (36,000) and two groups of canoes (400 each).

Trained warriors led by ali'i fought to take over land of both living ali'i and the recently deceased.

Weapons of choice were elau the (short spear), pololu ihe (long spear), palau (cudgel), leiomano (club with sharks' teeth) and later guns. War and weapons would be put aside with the unification of the islands.

A clear picture of what Kamehameha did, and how he did it, emerges by looking at his travels.

- **1778, Hana** — Meets Captain Cook and discovers unique sticks that fire bullets. He has foresight to see their potential in battle.
- **1783, Hawaii Island** — Starts campaign to unify islands by unsuccessfully attacking Hilo.
- **1785, Hilo** — A new attack.
- **1788, Kauai** — Trades land he controls for guns, including a swivel cannon. Captures sailor John Young, kidnaps Isaac Davis and names them military advisors.
- **1790, Maui** — Fights near Huelo and uses cannon for the first time in Iao Valley. Blood and bodies clog the stream, giving the fight the name "Kepaniwai" (Damming of the Water). Leaves before conquering Maui.

- **1791, Hawaii Island** — Builds Puʻukohola Heiau temple to win support of the gods for his unification effort. Uses swivel gun and cannon to win the battle and conquer the island.
- **1792-94** — Period of Peace.
- **1793** — Befriends Capt. George Vancouver, who was also acquainted with beautiful, Hana-born Kaʻahumanu, a surfing partner who became the king's first and favorite wife. Vancouver gives Kamehameha cattle, sheep and goats. Kaʻahumanu along the way deserted Kamehameha, after he flirted with Kaʻahumanu's sister. Vancouver is instrumental in bringing the two back together.
- **1794** — Announces that Hawaiian people are subjects of Great Britain and under its protection. Great Britain never agreed, but Vancouver gifts Kamehameha with a sailing ship with a Union Jack sail.
- **1795, Maui and Oahu** — Destroys Lahaina, then conquers Maui, Lanaʼi and Molokai in February. Sails to Oahu and wins Battle of Nuʼuunu on the

windward side of Waikiki to control Oahu. Leader of Kauai eludes capture.
- **1796, Kauai** — Invaded Kauai for the second time.
- **1797** — Takes a second wife in Keopuolani, who bears him a son, Liholiho, who succeeds Kamehameha as king. Ka'ahumanu, though childless, would later rule as regent for the young Liholiho and become Hawaii's first "feminist," ending the kapu system that banned kane and wahine (men and women) from eating together.
- **1802, Maui** — Fleet lands in Maui to prepare to invade Kauai again. A storm overwhelms warriors and ends expedition.
- **1803, Honolulu** — Fleet sent to new harbor and headquarters there. Kamehameha believes the Oahu harbor is better for loading ships (Lahaina Harbor was too shallow to permit docking of sailing ships). Becomes a trader, taking over the lucrative sandalwood trade and sending woods to China in exchange for worldly goods.

- **1810** — Completes unification by acquiring Kauai by agreement with the ali'i Kaumuali'i without a fight.
- **1812-19, Kohala, Hawaii Island** — Returns to birth island. Engages in his favorite pastimes of surfing, swimming, fishing and growing taro. Dies in 1819.
- **2012, Front Street, Lahaina** — Kamehameha images grace annual parade. Each Kamehameha Day, Pa'i riders on the former King's Highway pass within yards of where Kamehameha the Great once surfed, lived and enjoyed the King's Taro Patch.

Kamehameha, in a sense, was a man before his time. He recognized immediately the merits of western technology (guns, for example, which he rarely used).

He lived in three geographic areas like modern day corporate types, learned a foreign language (English) and created what would become one of the world's most progressive monarchies. Add every thing up, and no wonder he is called great.

DANCERS AND SINGERS
The Hawaiian Islands
Queen with a Uke, Hawaii Calls, and Slack Key Guitars

For centuries these islands have resonated with dance and the sound of chants, the ipu and the drum. Westerners' fascination with hula began early starting with Captain James Cook himself, "discover" of islands he named after the Earl of Sandwich.

Much later, missionaries frowned on hula and some tried to ban it. After hula went into decline, King Kalakaua, the Merrie Monarch, embraced it and brought it back.

Hula flowered in the last century when dancers like kumu hula (hula teacher) Emma Sharp who studied under a wahine who was a royal court dancer brought it to the troops in training or on R&R during World War II.

Others taught the traditional dances as well and Sharp brought it to virtually every new hotel that sprang up on the new Ka'anapali Beach Resort on Maui.

Music in the beginning came in the form of a chant accompanied by with the drum, the ipo.

The classical guitar appeared in the 1800s, brought by cowboys from Spain and Mexico to round up cattle for King Kamehameha III. The ukulele then made its way to the islands more than a century ago brought by two Portuguese instrument makers who sailed to Hawaii to work on the sugar plantations.

Soon even Lili'oukalani, queen of the Hawaiian nation and perhaps the only monarch in history to compose widely performed songs still sung today, helped popularize it.

Then at the turn of the century the steel guitar debuted. And finally came Kiho'alu (meaning loosening of keys), the slack key guitar that has become so popular today its players have won numerous Grammys.

As the new instruments thrived, those who played and sang with them did too. Not long after ukuleles and guitars became popular, scores of Hawaiian musicians in search of higher wages found gigs on the mainland.

The longest run was 45 years at the old Lexington Hotel in far away midtown Manhattan. There, a rotating series of dancers and singers handpicked by the impresario after visits to the islands enchanted thousands of New Yorkers.

Across the country, dozens and dozens of dancers and musicians performed in clubs like the Hawaiian Hut, Don the Beachcomber, Trader Vic's with a few of these clubs continuing to this day from Miami Beach to Las Vegas to LA.

For 40 years beginning in 1935, a national radio program called Hawaii Calls brought the mellow tones of the distinctive steel key guitar (sometimes called "the old music") to 750 radio stations around the world. Millions fell under the spell of songs of aloha and Hawaii.

Dozens and dozens of dancers and musicians performed in clubs like the Hawaiian Hut, Don the Beachcombers, Trader Vic's, with a few of these clubs continuing to this day.

And in the modern era musicians reached out to thousands more, first through 78 records, 45's, albums, CDs, iTunes and You Tube.

If you are in Hawaii, chances are the guitar and ukulele played by the famous or not so famous will be appearing at a venue near you — big places like the Blaisdell Center or the Maui Arts and Cultural Center, in famous

restaurants like Duke's on three islands, or at the tiniest cafe with a few tables.
Partake whenever you can. And sometimes, prepare to be amazed at the artistry and sounds.

NORM BEZANE, a former writer for Business Week magazine who visited Maui for 27 years beginning in 1969 before taking up residence in 2001, began writing the "Beyond the Beach" column for Lahaina News in 2006 and has now completed more than 150 profiles of the remarkable people of Maui.

Bezane's career has the shape of a pair of bookends. Beginning in journalism and then moving into the public relations profession in 1966, he served a variety of corporations and clients for 40 years. In life's home stretch, he now writes once again as a journalist.

In 2008, he performed the rare trick of being recognized for his work from Hawaii chapters of both the Society of Professional Journalists and the Public Relations Society of America.

Bezane writes from the perspective of a curious newcomer to the islands and not as an expert on the culture. From the unique point of view of an "outsider," he feels it is a privilege to learn and to acquire new understanding.

Bezane's previous books include "Voices of Maui: Natives and Newcomers," Maui for Millions, and a history, "The Incredible Journey of Underwriters Laboratories.

ACKNOWLEDGEMENTS

TO: Sara, Foley and Conor Bezane, the joys of my life and my frequent companions in paradise. And to Maui, for its unique ability to nurture its native born and attract adventurous, remarkable people, including those willing to share their stories here.

Special thanks to those who reviewed the final manuscript, especially the very knowledgeable Kahu David Kapaku who fine tooth combed the words for accuracy, good friends Dawn and John Balog, Debra Caswell and George Lavenson.

And to Mark Vieth, able long-time editor of Lahaina News whose knowledge of the island and its people has helped keep my columns relatively free of error.

Finally, once again to our lively dog Kea ALOHA, who chewed up a few pencils but once again did not eat the manuscript for breakfast, and for that matter, lunch or dinner.

"Voices of Maui books available at some local store in Maui as well as at http://voicesofmaui.com and amazon.com

FEEDBACK AND DIALOGUE

Comments. Readers are invited to send comments to the author at norm@mauicommunicators.com.

Blogs. Updates on Maui happenings can be found on my blog, voicesofmauitalkstory.com with almost daily posts as this is written.

Web Site: http://voicesofmaui.com

New columns. The newest Voices of Maui columns can be found at http://lahainanews.com

ALOHA

Made in the USA
Charleston, SC
03 September 2013